That One Who Loves The Universe

A modern tale of setbacks, second chances and spiritual enlightenment.

by

Sean Patrick

THAT GUY WHO LOVES THE UNIVERSE

This edition is published by That Guy's House in 2016

www.ThatGuyWhoLovesTheUniverse.com

© Copyright 2016, Sean Patrick

Table of Contents

A Note From The Author

Hello. My name is Seán and I love The Universe.

But we'll get to that.

First, welcome to my book.

Over this adventure together I'm going to share a story with you. It's not a long story but one that means an awful lot to me. It's a story about how my life changed.

Together, you and I are going to travel to one of the world's most life affirming cities. Along the way, we'll stop at midnight beach parties, eastern meditation retreats, and run into some unfamiliar religious rituals while in the company of a few extraordinary individuals. I'll tell you about how I found wisdom in mosques, five star hotels, white sandy beaches, and weird and wonderful coffee houses.

This story takes place when I was twenty-two after I spent more than a few too many years suffering with the *blues*. Maybe it was anxiety, insecurity and depression

1

and maybe I suffered with the same worry and feeling as so many do; *what am I doing with my life?* Truth was that nobody knew what was wrong with me, including me.

Either way I had to make a change.

I wanted this book to be as authentic as possible so in order to do that I have to welcome you into the world of my uncensored head. *Disclaimer:* there are dark corners, bright corners, self-obsessed corners and loving corners. I hope that you can forgive my occasional outburst of emotion and tendency to spend too long in my own head. I hope you see this book as somewhat of a diary entry; uncensored, imperfect, personal and most of all honest.

I would like to explicitly point out that this is a work of memoir and a true story. However, in addition to the unavoidable unfortunate flaws in memory, to serve the purpose of a narrative I have sometimes compressed time and events and have changed the names of the people in this book in order to protect their privacy. Except for *Moose* – whom I actually called Moose.

Finally, throughout the writing of this book I was tempted (and often advised) to make this book a more traditional *self-help* book filled with exercises and tools; though I personally read such traditional self-help books from time to time I have decided not to do that in this book. It is my hope and intention that you will take from this book what you see fit and be able to infuse its lessons into your life in your own way if you choose to do so. If not, it is my wish that just by enjoying the narrative of this book you will feel changed inside. Even if only a little.

So, I invite you to come with me on this journey. Overall, this is a story of how I got my head straight, and for me, and for most of us that is no small thing.

Let's begin.

Chapter 1

Anxiety is a form of art

I'd like you to come with me to the city of Liverpool, England. Enter a back-street apartment building, travel up two flights of stairs and come through a wooden door on your right. Then follow the beige carpet up the corridor and enter the bedroom on your left. There you'll find somebody hiding under the bedcovers scared to face the day because they are completely plagued with a self-loathing hangover.

That person was me.

Though I can't recall everything exactly, I know now that I was suffering from the universal epidemic of just not feeling good enough; feelings of low self-worth and emotional instability.

You could say I was suffering with the *blues* and I'm sure any psychologist at the time would have said I was depressed, anxious or clinically stressed, however, the truth was that nobody knew what was wrong with me, including me.

I felt sick, like having a hangover but one that was caused by a constant stream of self-hating thoughts.

I felt very much alone at the time, but I realise now that I wasn't the only one plagued by this crap. And for many people, it's unfortunately still going on. Just being *alive* in this day and age is more than most of us can handle.

What's life like for the majority of us?

We want things now. We download them fast. We drink our coffee on the go. We seem to worry incessantly and at the end of the day it seems like we've just run around in a circle. We go back to square one where we can't fall asleep until after midnight but still have to wake up at 7 a.m. to fuel our bodies with another cup of coffee and get on the endless merry-go-round again.

Sooner or later the "smarts" we received from our university education seem to pay off and we realise that this is not how we thought life would be. But we just don't have time to sit and process our thoughts because we are too busy and exhausted.

We frantically ask ourselves: *What's next? What's quick? What can I achieve?* Essentially, what I believe we are really asking is; *What can I do so I don't have to feel this pain?*

It's not long before we find something to numb the pain a little; fancy cocktails, sex, new clothes, and another qualification (just to name a few). I've experimented in them all. Might help for a while, but eventually we arrive at the stop in our lives where we were headed the entire time– *anxious as fuck.*

Like I said, I can't recall everything exactly because my early twenties seemed to be a blur of confusion and awkwardness, but what I can recall in detail is a time when my life held a very unforgiving mirror up to my face. This particular experience brought me up-close-and-personal with some very unpleasant truths about myself.

Thankfully it happened in class and style – *at a Beverly Hills Pool Party.*

WELCOME TO HOLLYWOOD!

Being from the UK I had only ever dreamed of having the chance to visit California. The life of the fabulous and famous was actually a fascination of mine in my teen years due to the overdose of celebrity television and my unhealthy addiction to the E! Network. I had not long finished university when I was invited to take part in a motivational training program that took place in Los Angeles. I was over the moon with excitement.

I mean – *I was going to LA.* I must have been real hot shit!

I connected with an old friend who lived in Downtown LA and we created an agenda for my trip that went something like this:

1. I would attend my training program.

2. We would indulge in LA by visiting the hottest bars and restaurants and afterward, we would cruise for celebrity sightings in Hollywood.

Before I knew it, my dream vacation had arrived. I bought a pair of designer jeans. I put on my mirrored sunglasses. I boarded my plane.

Californ-yaaaaaaaaahhhhhh.

Accordingly, my plan fell into place and after an exciting weekend of inspiration at my program, I hit the L.A. scene. I strolled along Rodeo Drive, even though I couldn't afford to buy anything and soon sought out the best bar in town. And I took an unusual amount of photographs of palm trees.

Palm tree on its own. Me in front of a palm street. Me behind a palm tree. The list goes on.

Just when I thought this entire LA buzz couldn't get any better, a bombshell was about the drop. Due to an extremely loose connection (a friend of a friend's friend), my L.A. acquaintance had landed us an invitation to a Pool Party in Beverly Hills at a Hollywood director's house.

Holy Shit!

Just a few hours later I arrived at the Kodak Theatre in Hollywood where a skinny guy with ironic hipster-looking thick black spectacles greeted me. He stood in what could easily be construed as a bitchy pose with a clipboard in his left hand. He gave me a good-old-fashioned judgmental look up-and-down and pursed his lips in loathing.

I began to feel slightly out of place. Among the sea of Dolce, Prada and Fendi, I felt slightly underdressed. I was beginning to feel inferior and despite the fact my friends back in England might have been jealous of this opportunity, I began to feel awkward.

"Are you on the list?" the guy with the clipboard asked me sternly.

"Erm…erm…yeah…I should be," I managed to reply.

"Name?" he ordered.

"Seán," I said. "I'm from the UK."

I have no idea what difference it made that I was from the UK, but the words came flying off my tongue anyway.

Once again I got the look; a drawn-out stare up and down and that callous pursing of the lips. His eyes eagerly scrolled down the page and I could tell he didn't think my name would not be on the list and he would be able to assert his air of importance by turning me away.

"Oh yes, here you are," he said as a cynical smile came over his face.

Flippantly pointing his hand to a black limousine, he ordered my friends and me to take a seat in the vehicle so we could be driven to the party. Of course, we did as we were told.

The limousine experience wasn't remotely what I had expected. Though these things are designed for you to have excess extra legroom we did not experience such luxury as a dozen of us packed into the car like sardines and a joint began to get passed around.

I was not disappointed at the sight that greeted me when we arrived at the Beverly Hills mansion. I'm sure I don't need to explain to you just how extravagant a mansion in Hollywood is because every image that you are currently calling to your mind is likely correct: marble floors, grandiose statues, water fountains, ten acre gardens and an infinity pool. Check. Check. *Check.*

As I wandered around the luxurious gardens of the Hollywood estate, I was disappointed not to come across a single celebrity sighting. But I did become rather numb to the number of cocaine lines and bathroom threesomes. All of a sudden, I wasn't enjoying my California Dream so much. The more I wandered around all this extravagant estate, the more I began to feel empty inside. I thought;

Wasn't it the pinnacle to be invited to a Beverly Hills Pool Party?

So why did it feel empty?

I looked around at the other guests and realised that we were all avidly on the prowl for a temporary sensation of feeling a little better than our ordinary lives allowed us to feel. It was clear to me that we would do almost anything to escape the feeling of not being good enough and experience a hint of self-worth, even if only for a brief moment.

Granted, some of us were looking for the escape in drugs, some through sex, and others, like me, were looking for it in the mere form of a party invitation. I felt a gut-wrenching sensation as I realised that I had lost the bet. I had to admit to myself that I had gambled for a feeling of ecstasy and had lost. Instead I was left feeling not much better than the dregs of my drinks floating in my red plastic cup.

I realised in that moment: *This world is crazy. This shit is insane and I'd sooner sit down and face up to some unpleasant truths about myself than search for scraps of self-worth at a pool party.*

I headed back to England just a few days later and decided that there must be more to life. Forgive the cliché.

But what exactly? And where the hell was I supposed to find it?

BEING AN ANXIETIST

I've coined a word that I'd like you to keep in mind … *Anxietist*. An anxietist is a person who practices the art and science of anxiety, worry, nervousness and unease.

If you are someone who has experienced anxiety, or just mere awkwardness, you know it feels a little like being followed by a voice. This voice knows all of your fears and insecurities and uses them against you. At first, it's just a voice in the background but soon it becomes the loudest voice in the room and the only one you can hear. Though at first, you might seem to be able to function while being followed by the voice, it doesn't give up. Soon it stops you from doing the things you want to do and no matter how much you want to shut this voice up, you can't stop listening to what it has to say.

At the end of the day, we have good reason to be anxious if we are alive on planet earth today. It's not hard to take a glance at the world and feel drastically mediocre and begin to crumble with fear and anxiety. When we were young, we were taught that anything was possible and we believed it. But now we spend a few too many days feeling inferior because we're terrified of living just an *ordinary* life. We treat the word *average* like it's a swear word. Slowly but surely we acquire feelings of self-loathing, constant worry, insecurity, depression, fear and social anxiety.

But yet, when we were born, we were naturally uninhibited and brave. *So what happened?* How come we abandoned our courageousness in exchange for self-doubt? We deserted the possibility of peace for the assurance of feeling frightened. Growing up in this world, we were not trained to remain peaceful, calm and loving. No, instead of that, as we grew up in school and university, we were trained to be in competition, expected to be the smartest, the strongest, the fastest, the best-looking, and the bravest. When we went off in pursuit of these lofty aims, we may have achieved success only to find ourselves asking, *"Is this it?"*

Yet we've all had moments of pure joy. A time when, as far as we were concerned, the world had stopped and we felt nothing but hysterics. *But then what happened?* Most likely the moment passed and we went back to our customary ways, never to forget that, once upon a time, we lived in pure ecstasy, no matter how slight or short that time was.

What we fail to believe is that we deserve to have that feeling of happiness more often, instead of merely settling for short bursts of joy in between long dry marathons of fear, anxiety, and boredom. If you're like me, then you've had a thought containing one simple message: *You deserve to be happy.*

Don't kid yourself, you've had that thought and I understand that it's a brave decision to admit it.

Seeking out the connection with your true self is not easy, but it's worth it.

Drinks & Doubts

Back in Liverpool I had made plans to meet my friend Olivia for a few cocktails. Olivia was born in New York and had grown up in London, England. She was raised in a wealthy family, travelled the world, and in my mind, she was that Bohemian wild-child that every twenty-something wished they could be.

Our paths crossed at university where we both studied for our theatre degrees. Olivia had known me since I was 18 and like many of my close friends, she was aware of some of the burdens I troubled myself with. However, Olivia always had a unique way of not feeling sorry for me. She was too smart for that. And there was also no judgement from Olivia. She was too wise for that too. Finally there was no pressure from her either. She was too gentle for that. Instead she would always acknowledge the ways we were both living a good life and doing the best we could.

This free-thinking attitude made her able to sit calmly in her chair, make jokes with strangers, and overspend money because she was having a lot of fun.

Damn I envied her.

It was clear from a million miles away that she didn't live in her worries, fears and doubts. Instead she enjoyed her life. Clearly, Olivia was not plagued with the burden of social anxiety, awkwardness and feelings of prolonged discomfort.

We ended up making a great pair of opposites as we sipped our drinks at the bar. Olivia was so relaxed, calm, and laid back. And there I was, so filled with self-loathing that the idea of even merely existing within a public space was distressing.

I was smart enough to know that I was more than just shy. Whatever I was dealing with was disrupting my whole life and I didn't know how to stop it. In other words ... I was constantly *inside my head.* Never free from thought. Never free to *just be.* In fact, at that time, I couldn't remember the last time I had simply sat and allowed my life to just *be* and enjoyed a damn cup of coffee without experiencing a damn existential crisis.

I put on my rehearsed courageous act and played the part of myself that was absolutely fine; free from affliction (the Apple Martini helped). I really pulled off putting on a great act; maybe it was my theatre degree or maybe anybody who is socially stunted learns a few acting skills but I had mastered a few ways to seem as if everything was fine when I was subject to a incessant internal monologue from my inner anxietist.

THE BATHROOM FLOOR MOMENT

We've all heard of the famous bathroom floor moment, that rock-bottom incident which brings us to our knees. Mine came on a summer's afternoon not long after my outing with Olivia. I remember feeling like a total self-help cliché. I had read the how-to books, watched the DVD's and attending the seminars and I still would have given anything to be free of my compulsive inner critic. There was no doubt about it: my head was spiralling out of control and my problems were not something that could be fixed by a *how-to* program.

I was working at a museum in Liverpool at the time and I had once loved my job there. I was in charge of engaging young people with the exhibitions and I knew I was lucky to have landed such a creative job fresh out of university. For a long time, I treated this job with my full respect and gave it my complete enthusiasm by pouring my heart and soul into all of the projects I was coordinating. I often worked late into the night because I just loved being there.

However, as a consequence of my on-going personal drama and the damned self-loathing, I had become dispassionate about this job. My office grew dull and so did my enthusiasm. I felt anxious for a freer more light-hearted version of myself to re-awaken. I longed to spend one more night with the version of myself who wasn't overly consumed with the file in my head labelled, "Look how much has gone wrong". By this stage, I had formed the conclusion that I was downright awful. Feeling sorry for myself on a regular basis and playing the first-world-problems game to win.

Maybe I should just disappear? Maybe there was a way I could check-out of my life without causing any drama or stir, and spend as long as I needed to get my head in order.

AN UNEXPECTED INVITATION

I have to admit I'm usually the first person to roll my eyes when somebody begins to tell me all about *how The Universe gave them a sign.* But to abandon this part of my story right now would be like trying to attend an AA meeting and not telling the 'rock-bottom' part. So here is my story of *that* moment.

I was aimlessly *Googling* on the computer in my office when I noticed my breathing became very shallow. I drank from my big bottle of water and then struggled to take at least one deep breath. I caught a reflection of myself in my computer monitor and abruptly made a decision: *I didn't want to be here anymore.*

I wasn't being dramatic and I didn't want to die. All I knew was that I had to get out of my office and more importantly I had to get out of my mind, a place where I had became so *uncomfortably* comfortable that I was blind to the idea that there could be anything more. Maybe a psychologist would have said that I was having a textbook panic attack but honestly, it felt more like I was having a huge argument with myself. It was less panicky and more like that moment when you just eventually lose it with someone. I was finally blurting out all of the things I had usually not wanted to say to myself and I was not holding back one bit.

Escaping from my office I was carelessly not acknowledging my co-workers or the pedestrians on the street or the traffic. It felt as if someone had a gun to my back, cleverly concealed behind my coat so that nobody could see, and with my complete co-operation, I was being forced home to my bed for what I expected would be another lengthy session of self-hatred.

I reached a small cobbled road and glanced both ways, stepped off the pavement to cross the street heading home. Once my two feet began to cross the cobbled street and the fresh air started filling my lungs, something subtly but surely began to happen. I felt the sunshine on my face, and my life held a necessary intervention which called a halt to my rioting thoughts, replacing them with one simple message: *"Seán - Stick around long enough for something good to happen."*

Okay. Let's pause here for a second so I can ensure you understand the profundity of what just happened. Yes, I know. It does sound a little surreal. But before you think that the skies parted and an echoing voice of God spoke to me from above then think again. This message was given to me in the way it *had* to be given to me; *hardly at all but undeniably so.* All I knew was that this one thought was placed in my mind with such velocity that I couldn't ignore it.

In the short five seconds it took to cross the cobbled street, it felt like I'd been through an eternity. By the time I'd reached the pavement on the other side, I had officially been busted by my own life. It had finally broken me down to a point where I could not lean on the crutch of mirrored sunglasses or designer jeans anymore, nothing could disguise me any longer. I finally realised that I needed to *chill the F out.*

After all why was I so stressed and worried all of the time?

I was equally a victim and an active participant in my drama.

I made it home without anything, else drastic happening. Maybe life might just be worth living after all.

***

Buuuuuzzzzzzzzz!

The unpleasant sound of the doorbell to my apartment rang. It was my very close friend Marie. She would visit me about three times a week. The reason Marie was such a close friend was because whenever she saw that I was self-sabotaging again, she brought it to my attention. It's sometimes refreshing to know that somebody can see right through you. It means you can stop pretending.

On this night, Marie bravely marched into my living room and began to fix her hair in my mirror. Marie made herself at home when she came to visit me, which I always appreciated. I started to make her a cup of tea in my kitchen and it wasn't long until she turned her head to look at me and courageously announced that she had been offered a job; a very exciting job that was going to fulfil all of her creative needs whilst giving her the chance to explore a new and exciting place.

Huh?

Oh yeah, the job was based in a city I'd heard very little about; Hong Kong.

"Hong Kong?" I gasped, "You're going to live in Hong Kong?! Hong Kong?!" I was blown away by her news that she was moving to another continent.

"Yes, babes," she replied with such enthusiasm.

Babes being our choice term of endearment for one another.

There wasn't enough sugar I could put in my coffee that would compare to the extreme wake-up call I got whilst listening to my friend's bold statement.

I didn't allow my mind to think of any reason to disapprove of her plan and I fought the urge to argue for my own limitations, listing all the reasons I should stay in my own rut. Instead my mouth opened and a question just came flying out: *Can I come with you?*

Confessions of an awkward twenty something.

So before we begin the story of my escapade let me just conclude this chapter on a few important notes. Here's the honest truth; I don't know how to live a life completely free from my feelings of insecurity and absolute exclusion of the thoughts in my head. I'm not there yet. But I'm definitely a lot further along than I used to be.

The first thing I can recommend for overcoming those unpleasant feelings in the moments where you feel lost and not enough (and I shall be offering a few other suggestions through the book) is to absolutely stop all of your self-criticism. Stop criticising yourself for how you look, stop criticising yourself for what you've achieved, and stop criticising yourself that you haven't done enough. *Absolutely stop it.* You are enough, you do enough, you have enough, it's all enough.

Just pretend to believe this at least for now. Fake it at first if you have to.

The second thing that really helps to overcome insecurity is to stop chasing approval like you're a scavenger looking for scraps of meat. We strive to be praised, recognised and appreciated by others, I know, it's natural. But have you noticed yet that there is no end to this? Even if you get someone's approval for a millisecond, you can't guarantee that person's approval the next day, and the next day and the day after that. If you try to keep up this scrounging for approval all the time, it's a sure recipe for exhaustion.

Instead, consider for a second, what do you actually get when someone approves of you?

I'm not trying to catch you out here, but the truth is you don't really get much. In fact, other than perhaps a slight lifting of your mood, you get nothing besides another scavenger hunt for the next scrap of approval out there.

And you know one more really good tip to keep a level head is to keep a list of the people whose opinions matter to you. I first heard this piece of advice from the wonderful Brene Brown, a best-selling author who wrote a book called *Daring Greatly* and many others. She says that she carries around her list in her purse. It's a sure-fire way to remember whose opinions matter to you. By doing this you will no longer care what your neighbours think, what your taxi driver thinks, or what your co-worker thinks.

And before I give every negative feeling a bad rap I'll finish by saying that we all feel a whole lot of things and there is no way that you're always going to feel good. I'd hate to offer you a collection of platitudes that make false hope and promise but I can offer you a few kind words about the ugly monsters that live inside of our heads. First, it's invisible. Thank God for that. You don't have to walk around with the T-shirt that says, *"Hello, I'm insecure."* And second, it's a wonderful reminder that tells you that something is out of line. So accordingly I hope you go forward with your life, get it wrong and maybe fall down or make a fool of yourself, who cares?

Maybe nobody is looking, anyway?

NOTES TO SELF;

1. Take a risk.

2. Listen to your inner voice.

3. You may think there is no hope but there is always hope.

4. Be willing to leave what is comfortable and familiar.

5. Get out of your own damn way.

Chapter 2

Miracles and mayhem often look the same

Like the majority of people, I don't like it when my life begins to drastically change. One moment I find myself with my feet up binge-watching TV box sets and the next day, I find myself preparing to move across the world to find a new home in Southeast Asia. This would be a mind-fuck for the most stable person in The Universe, so it was a sure thing that I wasn't handling it very well at all. Ever since I had said yes to my friend Marie in the kitchen, the decision seemed to be taken out of my hands: a flight was booked, my apartment notice had been handed in, and I began to wrap things up at my job.

There was no point fighting against it because it seemed that this was going to happen whether I liked it or not. I said goodbye to what I knew and drove down to London where I then said goodbye to my Mum – who was somewhat against my taking this trip. I boarded a 4 a.m. flight at London Heathrow Airport.

Cue: my arrival in the spectacular city of Hong Kong.

FINDING MY FEET

First things first; finding my feet. After a long plane journey and a pit-stop in Mumbai, I found myself jetlagged and confused in the *Tsim Sha Tsui* district of Hong Kong on a street called Nathan Road. I knew that Hong Kong was the perfect place to have an Eastern adventure. It's where the East meets the West so I could have all of the fun of trying exotic foods, sleeping on the beach, and learning to meditate without the fear of accidently ending up in a Thai-like-prison.

Being in the middle of a foreign city and finding yourself unaware of the simplest of facts such as what direction was left or right feels a little like trying to rollerblade whilst on crutches - *well I assume.*

I wanted a cup of coffee but I had no idea where to get one. I would have loved to have a nap but I didn't have a bed to sleep in. I wanted to call home but I didn't even have a phone yet.

Around me I saw a pandemonium of busy business commuters, awkward tourists and experienced travellers. They all went about their duties and responsibilities (or lack thereof) seamlessly against a backdrop of smog and high-rise buildings. Neon lit signs in Cantonese decorated the skyline while double-decker buses glided slowly through the congested roads. Business men who were talking on their mobile phones walked in a straight line at a strict and consistent pace while at the same time, hesitant tourists dodged out of their way in an impeccable sort of dance, never causing a collision. People freely crossed the road without waiting for a 'walk', 'don't walk' cue. The entire scene looked like a well-rehearsed synchronised swim team was performing it.

I was yet to learn where I would fit into this completely coordinated chaos. At first glance, I knew I have been able to forgive myself quickly if I had just turned around and gone home.

But then again, what was I really expecting? When I signed up for this exotic and divine voyage, I had imagined myself chilling on the beach, reading great books, and I automatically assumed that I'd *find myself.* I didn't imagine that I would be protecting myself from a hundred incredibly eager Indian entrepreneurs, cheerful men all holding their business cards so close to my face that I could barely catch my breath or take a step forward.

"You want copy watch, sir?" one of them offered with a smile. "I make you niiice fitted shirt?" another offered. "You need place to sleep – I know good hotel, you come with me, yes?" another man said politely while simultaneously picking up my suitcase and quickly vanishing into the distance expecting me to follow him. I was definitely feeling very *Eat, Pray, Love.*

I had expected to step off the plane onto Eastern soil and instantly have my heart filled with love and forgiveness. *Wasn't that what travelling to Asia was about?* You know, so you can tell people back at home that, "I'm travelling and it's changing my life." Turns out that this first-world-problem point of view was untrue. Instead I was thrown into a culture shock.

At this point I didn't really have the time or inclination to be pondering the meaning of life; the mid-day air was sticky and clammy and I was pushing myself through the mob of businessmen and their business cards.

I was hot, sweaty, confused, and dumbfounded – and it felt kinda good.

I continued to chase after the man who had escaped the crowd with my suitcase. I assumed he knew where he was going because I had no clue. This was the perfect time to allow somebody else to take the lead because I can humbly say that I had no idea what I was doing or what was going on. Somehow, throughout all of this, my British manners came up on my blind side and I politely excused myself all the way through the crowd. *No, thank you. Have a great day. I'm sorry. Please, excuse me. No, thanks, I'm fine.*

As I left the street, I entered into a building called the Chunking Mansions. From the outside it looked like an innocent concrete block but inside it was fifteen floors housing Hong Kong's finest selection of Indian restaurants and the humblest of homes. It was more than that even: it was Hong Kong's most famous jungle, a ghetto of suspicious activity, culture and chaos.

Upon first arrival into this man-made-village, I could tell that it was the type of place that the typical writer would have a field day describing – the distinct smell of Indian cuisine in the air, the maze-like arrangement of market stalls that went on for a confusing identical five blocks. There were about ten elevators that each only stopped at certain floors making it incredibly easy to end up on the fifth floor instead of the sixth.

I came to learn later that this building is rather infamous. Everyone in Hong Kong would either smile with glee at this establishment or run away with fear. The BBC once profiled this building, but many of its tradesmen refused to be interviewed due to their illegal immigration status or their illegal trade. I lost count of the number of times I was offered cocaine or marijuana just walking through Chunking Mansions on the way to my guesthouse. In defence of this wilderness, the noise, the fear, the smell, and the vastness of it all, I can happily say that it was the most unnerving place I've ever visited. Maybe, just maybe, that's what I needed in that moment.

The chaotic stampede of colour, culture, creativity was offensive to the version of myself, the one who would sooner make a cup of tea and curl up to watch television at home. I felt like I was being fed something new and delicious, but simply because I didn't recognise the flavour, my first instinct was to spit it out. It all felt like it was just too much – but too much of the good stuff; too much exploration, too much opportunity, and too much mysteriousness – exactly what I needed to get out of my rut.

***

There is a book I once read called *Wherever you Go, There You Are* by Jon Kabbat-Zinn. Though I have always understood this phrase it had never made more sense to me then when I caught my reflection in a steamed up mirror next to a mobile phone stall in the market at the Chunking Mansions. I looked exhausted and my skin was pasty white and just like old times, I took a moment to berate myself.

Like most people, I have a history of berating myself in the mirror. We don't talk about it but we all do it. It's like an altar where we arrange daily meetings with ourselves to pass on notes about all of the ways we're not good enough or worthy enough.

I know I'm not alone in living with an inner-critique in my mind, but this little demon drives me crazy with his endless list of all the ways I suck. If you could hear this voice in my head on any given day, you'd probably hear something like this: *"Hi, I'm your Self-loathing. In case you didn't know, you're not living up to your full potential. You should probably get in better shape and you definitely don't make enough money."*

I have had the honour – *or should I say dishonour* – of hanging out with all of these emotions and even their cousins. Sometimes self-loathing would show up uninvited and barge its way through my door demanding a cup of coffee and a long chat. Admittedly there have been other times where I have willingly invited self-loathing to my own dinner party, made space for it at the table, and even offered it a bed for the night (or the week, or the year).

I thought that by catching a plane and travelling 5,000 miles, I might find a window of feeling fantastic before my self-loathing caught up with me. *Nope.* It seemed to have taken the express plane and was waiting for me in Hong Kong from *Damn Day One.*

Our room in the mansions (and trust me, that word must be used ironically) was just big enough for Marie and I to fit in. One double bed and one single bed both squashed into a small box room with just a narrow walkway in between them. In the bathroom, the shower was placed over the toilet and sink making a visit to the bathroom an-all-in-one experience. We engaged in what seemed like gymnastics to climb over each other in order to push our suitcases under the beds before going out to explore the city, starting with our own building first.

INDIAN FOOD, ALLIES AND TRAPPED DOORS

Let me tell you something about me; when I'm happy – I'm ecstatic. If I have joy I am the first person who wants to share it with you. When I feel love it will spill over onto you at a velocity you couldn't even imagine. When I'm feeling overjoyed there is nothing I'd enjoy more than supporting you, loving you and caring for you. But when I'm knocked off my balance and I come to a feeling of such exhaustion and reduction then I simply have nothing to give. Like a big spender doesn't save any money for a rainy day, I had dried myself up of positive emotion in those blissful periods only to find myself broke and empty. The reason why I'm telling you this is because I don't want, at any point of this story, for it to sound like I was ungrateful for the opportunity I had been given in life. I was, at times, just feeling exhausted.

That night, my friend Marie seemed to be less taken aback by the shady surroundings we were in. In fact, she was eager to wander the back stairwells in search of great Indian food. The stairwells to this building were scary, like a scene from a horror movie; cold, concrete and abandoned and it offered the same feeling as walking alone in a graveyard late at night.

I have a history, and affliction, of assuming the worst too quickly. I imagine that it's part of an anxious nature but I feel very panic-stricken when I'm meant to *ride it out*.

Despite the fact that there was an Indian curry joint on every floor of the Chunking Mansions, we were both pretty adamant that we wanted to find a particular one that we had read about in the tourist guide called *Wakes Mess*. But it was not proving easy to find it.

Whilst experiencing a plentiful amount of juxtapositions, I found it difficult to even trust my thoughts, feelings or senses at that point so I just allowed myself to be led by my friend Marie. Every door we opened led to another dead end until we found ourselves so deep into this maze of the building that we couldn't even turn back if we wanted to. Door 101 - *Nothing.* Door 102 - *Another stairwell.* Door 103 - *A locked gate.* Door 104 - *Jackpot.* As we barged through that hundredth tattered wooden doorway, we came upon a dazzling scene of spiritual and religious treasures accompanied by the overture of the Islamic call to prayer echoing throughout the entire building.

At this point, Marie and I stepped out onto the mezzanine where we seemed to have an aerial view of a sacred moment in the room below us. Hundreds, if not thousands, of men fell to their knees and shovelled their hands into large basins of rice. There must be ten men to every bowl of food, each bowl the size of the basin of a wheelbarrow, each filled to the brim with yellow rice.

We were not oblivious to the fact that we may have somehow wrongly permitted ourselves these front row seats to a scene of spiritual devotion and that it was extremely touristy of us to see this as some kind of theatre. Despite the busy fast-paced frenzy going on outside of this mansion at the heart of the city, there are certain times of day when people put their business cards and everything and anything else aside for a time of worship. In fact, the gentlemen had a somewhat zombified look on their faces which said clearly to us, don't-you-dare-come-between-me-and-my-spiritual-practice. *Fair enough.* We were the spectators and we kept silent while watching in awe.

Suddenly, I felt the knot that had been growing in my stomach began to subside and the prevalence of fear was slowly overtaken by a feeling of curiosity. I began to ask myself a few silent questions. *Could I be exactly where I needed to be? Could this be here to teach me something? Will I be changed for the better because this happened?*

DO YOU BELIEVE IN MIRACLES?

I believe in miracles; those little magical moments in life where things change. I think somewhere deep down we all believe in miracles and are looking for them in our lives. Not necessarily the sea parting kind or the ones where a huge falling rock misses you by two inches (or a bird nearly shits on you), but rather those smaller moments when something inside of you shifts and you know that you've changed and your life has changed for the better. But I also believe in something else, probably more than I believed in miracles at this point of my life, and that is mayhem; that's a period of chaos, disorder and confusion where we have no idea where life is taking us and we don't like it.

I have come to learn that one of the great coincidences of life is that 99% of life's miraculous moments are preceded by a brief (or not so brief) period of mayhem, stress and anxiety. You've probably heard of the famous saying *a blessing in disguise?* Well, I do believe this happens, and I call this phenomenon something else: *a miracle disguised as mayhem.*

Let me put it this way; when you watch a film or TV series, you love the twists and turns in the storyline. Some of the best moments are where you thought everything was doomed but then somebody came to the rescue. Or even when you thought that the two main characters had finally got it together but then some fork in the road came up and kept them apart. Either way, you keep on watching because there is something extremely satisfying and poetic about the wonderful way that interesting storylines are woven around the lives of these characters.

So why do we fear the same kinds of twists and turns when they happen in our own lives? Those rich moments filled with mayhem that make for great T.V. tend to leave us running scared for our lives.

But let's not blame ourselves for being hard on ourselves because it's not easy to trust that there is something going on behind the scenes that will keep your life running and moving forward. In the midst or aftermath of heartache or moment of despair, the last thought you reach for is one that says, "Hey, it's OK anyway because life is working out for me." In fact, people around you might rightly think you were a little crazy to have such thoughts in the middle of a crisis.

But there is another side to the story here; what if you transferred your thinking and started to accept that miracles *could* arrive in your life disguised as mayhem? It's not about denying that bad things happen or that hard times do fall upon us sometimes, but there's nothing wrong with developing an inner confidence that somewhere, somehow things will eventually work out. It allows us to be able to relax just a little bit more and experience life from a peaceful point of view where we can likely make better choices.

Truth is, the mayhem in your life *can* serve you. Without a dose of it every once in a while, you may be tempted to allow everything to remain the same in your life: unchanged and unchallenged. But whenever a bit of mayhem rolls into your world, just watch and you'll likely find that life will push you in the direction of better things just down the road. Trying to run away from it or avoid it completely is a useless endeavour since mayhem is part of everybody's life at some point or another.

So what can we do to ease the pain when it's the worst? *Sit with it. Endure it. Breathe through it.*

Maybe a miracle is happening right now.

Notes to Self:

1. Sometimes blessings come in disguise. Stick around long enough to find the blessing.
2. Don't judge anything too quickly.
3. Be sure to take some time to enjoy some great Indian food.
4. Be willing to get a little lost.
5. It's okay to do something scary, but not to do something stupid.

Chapter 3

How to break up with your ego

The humidity in Hong Kong is fascinating. You will find yourself swimming though the moist air from 7-Eleven to 7-Eleven to catch the breeze of some icy air-conditioning. You soon learn to not bother styling your hair or to wear colours that show up sweat. The plus side to this is waking up to the sun shining through your window almost every morning and feeling the warmth on your feet from your floorboards as you make your morning trip to the kitchen. Being from England where it's cold more often than not this is not something I am taking for granted.

Once the initial chaos of culture shock settled down I was ready to fully begin my journey. The end of the settling in period was marked by the famous Hong Kong celebration of Mid-Autumn Festival (or Moon Festival).

43

Myself and my new found friends, all of whom seem to be making this Eastern adventure for some level of personal fulfilment, celebrate by eating dinner in a busy street market diner all sharing various plates of noodles, rice and meat. We pass the plates around and pose for pictures taken from our mobile phones. We later find ourselves around a beach campfire slowly dipping our toes into the freezing sea and daring each other to eat the traditional food of Mid-Autumn Festival; Mooncake - a recipe of red bean paste coated in sweet pastry.

I'll let you come to your own conclusions about this.

As midnight draws near we all hysterically dash through the city we know so little about to catch the last underground train to make it home.

As I quickly collapse into the hard seat on the train I realise that through all of the rushing around and experimentation with new food (some good, some bad, some ugly) I have not had time to listen to my hindering thoughts for a few hours or so. I'm not entirely certain at this point but I'm beginning to feel as if I could find some, if only a little bit, of happiness here.

One thing was for sure. If I was going to even attempt to have a happier life, I had to stop listening to that voice in my head that provided a damn running commentary of every situation. I could not see myself actually being able to enjoy my life unless I somehow got a handle on the wild critical thoughts that kept swimming around in my head.

As I looked out upon the Hong Kong skyline with its dancing lights shining in bright-pink, neon-green, and dark-red, I knew that an adventure like no other lay before me. I wasn't aware of what was going to happen but something inside of me knew that if I gave in to this whole experience then I would be changed for the better on the other side.

But for this to work, I needed to make a tough call. I had to break up with my *Ego*.

MY FRIEND AND FOE - EGO

You're probably familiar with the word *ego* and have read about it time and time again but don't fully understand it. If I may, let me refresh your memory in my own words; Ego is a tiny three-lettered word with huge consequences. Various definitions of this little word exist such as those coined by Freud, other psychologists and numerous spiritual teachers. The definition I like the most is that put forward by the metaphysical text *A Course in Miracles* which says that the ego is about 'wrong mindedness'; the voice in our head which speaks very loudly but doesn't utter truth.

This became more apparent to me one evening on the Hong Kong underground (train system known as the MTR). I soon began to find refuge here, as the air was cool and clean. Riding the train was at least a twice-daily necessity where I had to allow the air-conditioning to cool me and read a good book for the duration of my journey.

Bliss.

As I sat on the train contemplating how I voluntarily snatched myself away from my old life I became unnerved that nothing, and I mean *nothing,* around me was comfortable or familiar. Even my friend Marie that I had travelled with was more than often doing her own thing. I was completely anonymous in this wilderness; every stop on the train welcomed a few hundred more passengers in which not even a single one, under no circumstance, would know who I was.

I had to pause.

I had spent a good portion of my life equating myself with how I could be identified by the people around me. However, absent from this I guess I was just what I was - *a guy on the train reading a book.* Nothing more.

And this felt good.

I had been given the chance to shed anything familiar about my life and myself and only welcome back in the things I wanted.

For a brief moment on this train ride I was who I was without any story attached to it.

I got off the train at Prince Edward station and continued being just another nameless person in the world and began to wonder why I had never noticed before that there was such peace to be found in obscurity.

Just a thought, I told myself.

A FEW HOME TRUTHS ABOUT THAT VOICE IN YOUR HEAD

When you were far younger than you are today something happened that made you feel like you may not be *good.* Like most children in our world today, you were likely raised with a strong moral compass drilled into you, and you either felt good or felt bad based on how you were *acting and behaving.* Very few of us were given a sense of approval that was based on *who we were inside* as opposed to how we behaved or what we were achieving.

This isn't because you were raised by evil beasts or because the world is full of wicked people, but because this is the age old way. We were taught the same set of rules as our parents were; that if you did good, then you were good, and if you did bad, then you were bad and who we were had nothing to do with any of it.

And what did this teach us? *Fear.* Fear that if we didn't show up in the world the way we were taught to do, then we would be rejected. And that is a really scary thought.

Consequently we go in search of approval and acceptance; it seems to be part of our DNA. We listened very carefully to our thoughts to make sure that we never stepped out of line and consequently, sooner or later, we can become paralysed by our own thinking.

Unfortunately we can't go back and change that early conditioning and it's not necessarily a bad thing to be aware of your inner monologue but the problem is when we grow up and become adults and we are still in a constant search of approval and acceptance. When we do this and try to reject our inevitable imperfections we start to do some crazy shit.

It may manifest in your life a little like this:

You define yourself by either being better than or worse than other people.

You live on a constant merry-go-round of feeling good and then feeling crappy.

You will always want something and won't spend long being satisfied with anything you have.

You will believe that it's you against the world.

You will think that you don't have enough time.

You will always want to be right – even if it means being miserable.

You will sometimes think how much better you are than other people because of x; y or z.

You will not be happy but will always think that it's just one more thing you need in order to feel happy.

You will be exhausted at the end of every damn day.

A glamorous London-party-girl friend of mine once told me that living in this world constantly listening to your ego is exhausting and told me that it doesn't matter how long I listened for, it would still repeat the same old shit day in and day out.

I believe that ego should come with a warning label - *Beware of your over consumption of ego: it will cause you to chase one thing after another until you miss your entire life in the process.*

I was on the verge of having the most incredible time of my life; I had been given freedom, opportunity and adventure and I was still stuck listening to that voice in my head that kept a running tab of all of the ways I didn't quite measure up.

It can sometimes get to the point where you feel bad for even having an ego – that's a crazy thing some spiritual people tend to do - feel bad for having an ego. Feeling bad about having an ego is like feeling guilty for having legs, arms or your mind. It's there. It likes to come out and play. It says some crazy shit. End of story. *Well ... almost.*

MR. WONG'S CHINESE RESTAURANT.

If you look hard enough, *really* go searching, you'll come across a tiny outdoor Chinese restaurant in the Kowloon district of Hong Kong *called Mr. Wong's.* Truth was we didn't know what it was actually called but the owner, Mr Wong, had taken a liking to us and we got to know him on a personal level. There on in it was always just a trip to see Mr Wong.

Now I use the term restaurant loosely as you will sit outside on plastic stools around a low wooden table, but the food is so incredible and so cheap you won't care.

In an attempt to make new acquaintances in this wonderful city, I accepted an invitation to dine here with a group of expats, people like me who were from other countries but who were visiting or working here. It cost us less than about ten pounds for all the Chinese food we could eat and all the beer we could consume. I've never really been a beer drinker but that night I made an exception.

On this particular night, there were about ten of us and we were practically strangers. This is what you call an Anxiestist's worst nightmare. Making it a little easier for me to lean in to this social gathering was a beautiful English rose called Sophia who sat beside me.

I learned that Sophia and I had both studied and lived in Liverpool yet were meeting for the first time at this mysterious Chinese hole-in-the-wall eatery in *Mong Kok*. As

Sophia leaned in to speak to me, I noticed myself freeze up and become awkward, not quite sure how to react. Unfortunately this was classic for me, I had been hijacked by ego.

You might be familiar with what an ego hijacking feels like because in the middle of just an ordinary moment, you suddenly experience any or all of the follow symptoms, such as low self worth, awkwardness, a need-to-prove yourself, an unreasonable comparison to others, an exhibition of arrogance, and a feeling of anxiety. All sponsored by that voice in my head.

MY FAVOURITE PLACE IN THE WORLD

One of the first places I found solitude was at the Kowloon Park Pool. It was an outdoor paradise sheltered by palm trees and high rise buildings. I first came across this miniature slice of heaven accidently when I was walking late at night around the Tsim Tsa Tsui district and got lost. Surrounded by rocks, greenery and skylines, this aquatic utopia symbolised a tropical island under the stars.

I was walking with friends. They were less stunned by this public swimming pool and were rather stunned by my overreaction: *Can we go? Can we go?* I pleaded like a little school boy. I just wanted to plunge into the water. I don't know why but I've always felt peaceful when in water.

"Please, please, please, can we go swimming?" I continued to beg. I hadn't yet realised that I was a grown man and could simply go swimming alone if I so desired. That's a problem I often faced. I'd always found myself in constant need for permission from other people and the desire to have company through everything I ever did.

Though there were many more extravagant things on my bucket list one of mine was very simple; go for a cup of coffee on your own, order a drink and sit down. This may sound like a small task but I'd always dreaded being in my own company in a public setting. I can look back now and see that the voice in my head was massively out of control.

However, that night in Hong Kong, near the pool, I realised that I had to begin somewhere and decided to make a small step. I decided that I would go swimming alone and soon found myself swaying and floating under the Hong Kong stars and city lights. *Bliss.* The air was warm and the water was cool.

It was one of those perfect moments.

ONE SMALL STEP FOR MANKIND, ONE GIANT STEP FOR ME

As I lounged comfortably in the shallow end of the elevated smaller pool at the far end of the park, I begin to once again contemplate this thing called *ego*. I still wasn't sure if I fully understood it but I knew that I've suffered from too much of it.

It's fair to say that I've always been more interested in the Eastern and spiritual concepts of this thing we call *ego*, which as I have described already, is actually a sense of identity that is false. Often times we base who we are (our self-identity) on our personality, abilities and talents and our ego is quick to remind us that this is all that counts.

But what if who we are *went beyond all of that?*

I dried myself off and got dressed and started walking alone around the wonderful streets of Kowloon. Hong Kong really is a spectacle to see at night time. Anyone who has been to Times Square in New York will understand that there is something mesmerising about a parade of neon lights. The same way a firework display demands your attention, so does a beautifully lit city at night.

Amongst the giant neon Chinese characters for Hot Food, New Watch and Tailored Shirts, I saw a sign I recognised immediately: *Starbucks*.

Now I know there may be a few of you who want to judge me for consuming coffee from a corporate chain like this, and call me a bad spiritual person for drinking there. Perhaps you'd be more comfortable if I frequented an independent coffee shop to sip my espresso. But at this point in my story, I needed a latte and I was damn sure I was about to get one.

Where I get my drink from is not the essence of the story anyway. It's what I decided to do that's important - *go for a coffee on my own.*

One small step for mankind. One giant step for Me!

***

As you may have noticed I don't rely on fireworks and parting seas to acknowledge the presence of *something more* in my life. I take it in any form I can get it; a gentle nudge in the right direction, a hit of intuition or something I just *know* is a sign.

And on that day, my walking up to the counter of this coffee shop, asking for a Latte and then taking a seat solo was a damn sure sign of following a small nudge of inner guidance. I was always petrified to be with just myself and here I was taking a chance, not getting the order to go, but sitting down.

As I took my seat and like all my other messages from The Universe this one came to me as an inspiring thought; *"I'm going to show you a life so beautiful that you'll probably find it hard to remember what your life was like before".* And thus the classic journey toward enlightenment ramped up another notch and the next step was clear. The time had come.

I had to break up with my *ego* – well the ego of my understanding; that damn incessant and relentless voice in my head.

It was a time to be direct and firm and thus my inner conversation began.

Me: Hello.

Ego: *Hey there — have you noticed that everybody is staring at you?*

Me: No. I don't think they are.

Ego: *Yes, they are and if I were you, I would be feeling pretty self-conscious right now.*

Me: Interesting. I feel very much at ease right now.

Ego: *Really? Well ... have you seen how you look? You're a mess. And don't even get me started on how much of a failure you are because —*

Me: Listen. I'm sorry to interrupt you but I am no longer going to accept your invitation to feel crappy about myself. I'm not entirely sure why but I've accepted an offer to begin to imagine that there is something magnificent about me.

Ego: *But...but....but...*

Me: And I want to thank you for how you've always been there for me. I know you just want me to have more, be more, and do more, we've had some laughs, but I've come to learn that I can't be happy and continue to hang out with you.

Ego: *So what are you saying?*

Me: I think we should break-up. It's not you, it's me. I'm just in a different place right now.

Ego: *I'll be back.*

Me: Oh, I'm sure you will, and you're welcome to visit occasionally to spur me on to be my best. However, if you begin to harass me and torture me again, I will have to file a restraining order.

Ego: *So this is goodbye?*

Me: Yes. But I have no doubt I'll see you around.

KEEP A NEW KIND OF *Little Black Book*

For the first time since I could remember, I allowed myself to sit in my own company in that Starbucks for long enough to let my insecurities melt away. I breathed an immense sigh of relief and stretched my legs out.

Dear World - I feel like I've arrived.

It was small and subtle but everything I needed.

And then The Universe, in its divine wisdom, delivered another thought to me; *"You've come a long way, my darlin'. It's all going to be okay."* And with that I understood. I decided I was going to allow myself to be happy again. And that *was* a damn miracle.

Just as I began to exit the coffee shop, I wrote a mental note to myself; *"Dear Me, may you never forget that once-upon-a-time in an East Asian coffee house you made peace with yourself".*

You see, as far as I know there's no way of living a life completely free of ego – and you probably don't want there to be. You're always going to have thoughts and they are either going to make you feel wonderful or miserable. My advice is to just *accept it.*

Another thing you can do to get your crazy thoughts out of your head is to put them down on paper. This is extremely beneficial and it helps you really clear your mind. One way to do this is by writing a letter to your ego (or to your head) which documents all of the ways in which you are at war with yourself. This can be called an *ego journal.* When necessary, I write to my ego (to my head) either in the form of short memos or sometime long letters explaining why things need to be different.

Don't worry so much about keeping a notebook; use your phone or begin to jot it down on a scrap piece of paper – just get your thoughts out of your head and write it down. After all, you can't *meditate* it down. You can't *medicate* it down. You can't *drink* it down. You can't *shop* it down.

So do yourself a favour and write it down

At the end of the day, it all comes down to one simple game of truth or dare. Truth - *accept that you are a human being and there is nothing fundamentally wrong with you.* Dare - *to live your life knowing this.*

NOTES TO SELF:

1. Stop believing there is something wrong with you.
2. Say yes to social invitations; you just might make a new friend.
3. Go for coffee on your own.

4. Stop judging people. You are no better than (or worse than) the majority of people you spend time with.

5. Keep a Little Black Book to keep your ego in check.

Chapter 4
What Buddha and Beyoncé Have in Common

I'd like to tell you a story of Buddha & Beyoncé.

I am aware that it may be somewhat blasphemous and silly to compare a sacred religious figure to an international superstar. But stay with me because after you've heard my story I think you might agree.

It all began with a chance meeting at a Starbucks coffee house in central Hong Kong.

I sipped my new favourite drink; an Iced Green tea latte and flipped the pages of *HK Magazine* - a what's-hot-and-what's-not guide to the city that was mainly for tourists. I was waiting to meet up with some people who were interested in renting a 6-bedroom apartment just off Hollywood Road. It was a first come first served situation and expats were gathering in crowds to claim one of these bedrooms.

I kept my head in my magazine and was drawn to a two-page spread about a gigantic 100-foot Buddha that lived only one hour away on the island of Lantau.

I had to go.

'Hey, are you waiting to see the apartment near the Man-Mo temple?' a voice behind me asked.

I turned to see an American woman, hippy like, with ashy blonde hair that fell down past her waist.

'I am.'

'I know where it is, let's beat these guys and get there first!'

I jumped at the opportunity and followed this woman past street-food carts, Buddhist temples and cool-hipster-start-up business units and found myself down a back ally in front of a sixty-story apartment building.

I don't know why this woman chose to beat the crowd with me. But I'd come to question things a hell of a lot less since arriving in Hong Kong. I had simply learnt to go with it.

'We're here!' she said.

I was confused.

'I'm Lori.' she presented her hand for me to shake.

Lori and I entered the building and took a lengthy elevator ride to our floor. We were the first people there and swiftly signed our names on the dotted line.

We were officially roommates along with four other people who we hadn't yet met who were probably still hanging out at the Starbucks coffee house.

'Let's do something touristy!' Lori squealed.

I wasn't sure what to suggest, we were complete strangers and I didn't know my way around the city at all.

'Let's go and see the Big Buddha!' interjected Lori.

SELF-HELP AND EASTERN PHILOSOPHY

By now you've probably figured out my enduring love for Eastern philosophy and I freely own up to the fact that I am guilty of sampling from those traditions from time to time. One day, you might see me wearing mala beads or reading Ghandi's autobiography, while other times I might be sporting a red piece of string around my wrist and saying that I was exploring "the art of kabbalah".

Of course, I never meant any disrespect by any of this. I was just being guided to try new things, acting on the inkling that there was something more out there, and experimenting with the many different possibilities. I definitely drew one conclusion from my dabbles into various religious and philosophical practices and that was that peace and happiness were available to every human if they were willing to go in search of it. I know this belief is at the core of just about every self-help book available today, but I still think that there is a distinct difference between Eastern philosophy and Western self-help. When you read a lot of the customary style Western self-help books, it seems as if they are saying if you *try* hard enough, and *do* a certain amount of prescribed actions you will in turn achieve set goals, you will then find happiness.

Eastern philosophies seem to have a different view on the matter of happiness. In most of the works that I have studied it states that when you finally stop all of your doing, trying and striving, you will experience happiness that was there all along. The problem is not that there *is* something you need to do in order to feel happiness but that you *think* there is something you need to do.

THE BUDDHA AND BEYONCÉ PRINCIPLE

There is no greater place where the West and East meet than the marrying of Buddhism and Beyoncé. This might sound silly but hear me out.

Buddha isn't just the man that the religion of Buddhism is based around. In fact, the word Buddha is more of a title meaning, 'One who is Awake'. In a sense, it means someone who has woken up to reality. And many of you may have heard that the man we know as Gautama Buddha never claimed to be a God or a prophet. It is his presence and God-like-qualities that can make us think that way about him.

It's the same with Beyoncé. She has never claimed to be a God or a prophet either. It's just that her presence and God-like-qualities makes us think of her that way.

And if you have ever been to a Beyoncé concert you'll know that people respond to her like she is a God.

So you see, it's not such a crazy comparison is it?

And the similarities don't stop there. A main teaching of Buddha is the idea of enduring suffering, that we should stop running away from suffering, since it is an unavoidable human affliction that we all must endure at some point (and even embrace). I contemplated this philosophy while I was watching a Beyoncé documentary where she was asked about how wonderful it must feel to have the world at her feet. To my surprise, Beyoncé looked into the camera and made *what I thought* was a shocking confession: despite the fame, love and adoration from the world, *she also suffers.*

It's then what she said next that really got my attention. She said "when I'm scared, I allow myself to be scared. Stop pretending that I have it all together. Allow it. Accept it. Move on".

Her message was concise and universal, and I never forgot it even to this day. Fear happens. Don't bury it. Don't pretend it's not there. Allow it. Accept it. And move on.

So there it is my take on what Buddha & Beyoncé have in common.

Worlds apart but a lot closer than you may think at first.

TIME FOR A ROAD TRIP

Back with Lori we had commenced our journey to the Big Buddha on LanTau Island.

Despite the fact that there are a number of speedy routes to get to this landmark, my friend Lori insisted that we go via the bus through a route that included an almost deserted island in the middle of Southeast Asia. I slipped in and out of consciousness on the coach. Small villages replaced skyscrapers as we drew closer to Lantau Island.

I have a confession.

This trip was about more for me than some interesting photos for my Facebook page.

I wanted to give the Buddha a piece of my mind.

Not *necessarily* Buddha *per se,* but I wanted to confront some higher power with my anger and frustration. I felt I needed this monument of a higher power to answer for the way I felt. I was lost and confused at this point in my life and wanted to blame somebody for it. Other days I blamed my parents but today I had chosen Buddha.

Long story short; I was desperate.

I'd come to learn that desperation is not a particularly bad place to be when on the search for peace. In some ways, I think you almost have to feel some level of pain and anxiety before you finally fall to your knees and admit that you have no freaking idea how to handle life on your own.

I was there.

I'd fallen down and now was ready to get back up.

MEETING BUDDHA

We finally got out of the coach and arrived at what seemed to be an unlikely site for a pilgrimage. This was a man-made town that looked incredibly touristy and European. It looked to me like a Buddhist Theme Park with overpriced gift shops, pizza restaurants, and even a Starbucks.

I drank an iced latte and then enjoyed the lavish tours through the extravagant temples that led to the main attraction of The Giant Buddha.

As Lori disobeyed the "no photography" signs, I had alternatively, and some may say Britishly, decided to experience the temples a little more subtly.

I found myself standing small at the feet of gold statues of Buddhist Gods and Goddesses – at least that's what I thought they were. Without giving this too much thought I had a sudden impulse to *pray*.

Like on my knees.

I swear to God (or maybe I shouldn't bring him up right now) but this was a weird impulse to come over me. I mean, I've prayed before and many times on my knees (after all I was raised an Irish Catholic) but I just didn't expect to be called to do it on my own accord while in a Buddhist Temple.

Should I bless myself?

How do I begin?

Do I say 'Dear God'?

Or should I say 'Dear Buddha'?

Or are Buddhists so enlightened that they just begin their prayer?

Do they even pray in words?

Holy Shit! I've even turned praying into self-doubting commotion.

And just like that; I'd lost my 'Zen'. That's if I even had it in the first place.

Self-consciousness creeps in and I realise that I'm on my damn knees in front of hundreds of snap-happy tourists and my desire to pray subsides.

Operation Prayer and Enlightenment: Game Over!

***

I finally reached the top of 268 steps. I felt like I had officially worked out for the day. Maybe the real reason that people feel so enlightened in the presence of this statue was because they were euphoric from the exercise endorphins racing through their system after climbing that giant staircase.

Please forgive me; I know I may sound cynical sometimes but I'm really not. I had arrived at The Giant Buddha with respect and excitement. You can walk the entire way around the Buddha and look out for miles on magnificent greenery as well as go inside of the statue.

I was truly feeling joyful, having such a good time that I forgot the reason I came here: *to give Buddha a piece of my mind.*

Strangely I had forgotten how pissed off I was that I had searched for peace in the past and been let down. I had shown up for life all those time and life had not always showed up for me.

Once I remembered my real agenda, I composed myself and prepared to let it all hang out. I still had a lot of pent up anger and I was ready to let him have it.

Here it goes.

But I couldn't.

I tried again.

But it just wouldn't happen.

I called to mind some of the things that made me feel the most sad and hurt.

But no matter how hard I tried I couldn't seem to access that feeling of inner resentment and anger.

I searched for it.

I continued to call to mind all of the ways I believed I had been wronged. I remembered my sadness, my unhappiness, and my heartbreak. But it was a fruitless task because in that moment, for some reason unknown to me, I didn't feel angry, hurt or sad. In fact, I felt .... *grateful.*

I really wish I could explain it more or give you a step-by-step guide as to how I came across this sensation, but I didn't really do anything to achieve it. It kind of just showed up on my blind side. It was as if once I allowed myself to explore, I felt this feeling of peace come over me.

I didn't have to *do* anything. In fact, I had to stop doing everything and there it was - a little *peace.*

I learned that day that that's the way peace works; in order to get there, you have to stop trying so desperately hard to get there. It's not something you have to achieve; it's something you have to *allow*.

With that in mind I let out one giant exhale - *"hello peace, it's nice to see you again."*

THE TAI CHI CLASS

This is a good time to explore some other aspects of Eastern philosophy and it seemed to show up like this - *fluid and slow and feeling the energy between your palms.*

Yes, I'd decided to take part in a Tai Chi lesson on the pier in Kowloon.

I have to admit that I was only half-heartedly committing to my 'hand and weapon forms' due to a feeling of overtiredness from binge watching TV the night before. This 6am class definitely did not showcase my best efforts.

When you are performing Tai Chi in a large group on a public pier, you tend to become the object of many tourists attention as they walk by the pier with their bulky cameras around their necks. My ego was either getting a total kick, or totally embarrassed by being photographed by strangers.

When I first arrived at the class, the instructor greeted me with a humungous amount of glee and insisted that I stand at the front of the class. This was because in order to sneak my way into the class for free I had told him that I was a blogger and would love to do a piece on Tai Chi and spirituality.

I *did* eventually fulfil that commitment.

He himself was only about five-foot tall, and totally adorable, seeming to me to be about 140 years old.

Like many ancient spiritual practices, Tai Chi had become a rather trendy Western movement. It's almost fashionable to be spiritual and to take Tai Chi classes, however, the benefits based in its origins are by no means a fad.

Almost as soon as I began, I started to feel the energy in between my palms and the chatter in my mind began to die down.

I was sinking in.

I was in flow.

I was feeling at ease.

And then the instructor called it - Class Over!

What the hell? I thought. I stood in the fiery sun in disappointment. *I was just getting some fucking peace,* I thought. Then I laughed at myself. I realised that it was so like me to want things in this way: instant and easy. I used to say to friends that if there were a magic pill available called 'spiritual enlightenment'; I would be buying that shit in bulk.

***

I hadn't really considered that gaining a stronger connection with The Universe might actually take time, focus and training. As a product of my generation I wanted it quick, now and fast.

I collected my flip-flops from the pile of shoes gathered against the wall of the pier and I grabbed a notebook from my bag.

"Excuse me, my name is Seán," I told the instructor. "And I'd love to speak to you".

The old man was expecting me. He had a huge smile decorating his face. He put his arm around my shoulder and led me to a small brick wall on the pier.

"What does spirituality mean to you?" I asked.

"Tai Chi *is* spirituality," the instructor told me. "It's an ancient martial art that is good for your health. Tai Chi is also meditation – it's good for your mind. All of this is spiritual."

This made sense to me. After all, I was in search of a healthier mind for myself, so I pushed on. "But do you think that spirituality has a place in our modern world?"

"Yes. Tai Chi is both modern and ancient all at the same time," he explained. "It is very important that we bring spirituality into our modern world but it will take us until we are very, very old to truly feel enlightened, so that's why Tai Chi is good because it will make you live until you are very old."

What a good answer I thought, and I laughed to myself quietly so as not to appear rude. I felt a sense of elation at what the instructor just said. Maybe we weren't supposed to have it all together in out twenties and maybe we weren't even supposed to have it all together in our forties either. After all, hadn't it been my insecurity, my sadness and my own fear that brought me to this wonderful pier?

"But I want to be happier," I blurted out.

This time it was the instructor who giggled as if this was the most common thing anybody ever said. "Stand still – be very still," he instructed. "Allow your mind to be silent. When it feels right, open your palm wide and begin to move your arms. Feel the energy around you, in the air, and feel the life within your body. When you enjoy doing this as much as you enjoy searching for happiness, you will find your happiness."

He seemed quite sure. It seemed we had completed our chat, so I thanked him very much. As he walked away, I wondered did he mean that I should maybe put my search for happiness on hold?

That was the experience I had at the Big Buddha; a feeling of peace caused by the absence of something rather than the presence of something.

I felt a huge surge of ecstasy as I thought about the experience.

Enjoying the warmth and beauty, I turned and looked across the water toward the Hong Kong skyline that was standing proudly. There is something so distinctive about the Hong Kong skyline, especially with its wide variety of colours. It's like a celebration of every colour ever invented: various shades of luminous greens, hot pinks, deep purples, and electric blues, all painted across an epic army of strangely shaped skyscrapers. I had to admit that Hong Kong had charisma. It's a city steeped with personality and charm and I was growing more and more fond of being here every day.

ONE LAST STORY ON BUDDHISM.

As I close this chapter allow me to share an ancient Buddhist tale with you about an Indian Prince who once called a meeting with Gautama Buddha.

Buddha compassionately asked The Prince what he valued more, his worldly possessions or a sense of inner peace and happiness?

The Prince answered quickly and certainly - 'of course my worldly possessions, I love and enjoy my riches and romantic intimacies'.

Gautama did not disagree with The Prince nor invalidate his answer and simply asked The Prince to do him a favour - 'would you take just one hour of your time and go and sit under that tall tree over there and when you have finished can you please re-answer my question?'

'Of course' the prince replied.

He went and spent sixty minuets in silence under the tall tree and after his one hour of silence The Prince returned to Buddha and further insisted; 'I still believe that my worldly goods are far more satisfying'.

Okay', Buddha replied 'but could you do me another favour', he asked;

'Can you please go back to the tree and just sit there for another sixty minutes longer'.

The Prince agreed do what Buddha had asked of him and once again returned to the tall tree and continued in his meditation and was recalled to a beautiful memory of his childhood where he was playing sports with his father, the memory soon subsides and The Prince was left with the beautiful feeling, loosing all concept of the time, The Prince basked in his peaceful state.

Overjoyed The Prince began to contemplate the idea that happiness may not lie in his worldly possessions and just as The Prince began to process the belief that his joy was forever within him somebody tapped him on the shoulder, it was a masked man dressed entirely in dark clothing. The man got close to The Prince's ear and insisted, 'don't start to think that your joy is within you, your joy lies in your possessions and look how much pleasure your riches give you'. The Prince was taken in by this man's conviction and quickly exited his meditation and returned to his palace.

I share this story to point out how similar we all are to The Prince in this story. Our intentions are right and we are taking correct action, however, at the very last minute we are bailing out with what we think is a valid reason.

This is not because we are bad, lazy, wrong or entitled but because it is the age-old pressure of the world.

Below I share an exercise that can help us continue to sit under that tree for a moment longer; this exercise is inspired by the Buddhist (and Beyoncé) philosophy of accepting suffering.

THE BUDDHA (AND BEYONCÉ) EXERCISE FOR ACCEPTING SUFFERING

You don't need superpowers to deal with suffering, just the willingness to embrace it. Remember that Buddha was just a man and Beyoncé is just a woman

Suffering does not just mean deep grief brought on by death, infidelity or major loss. We also experience suffering when we get stuck in traffic, our phones run out of battery or you miss out on concert tickets.

To put it simply, we suffer when we argue with our lives.

If you're honest with yourself deep down you know what's causing you to suffer.

This is the time to create a safe space for yourself to finally release it.

knowledge

Being honest with yourself is the first step in dealing with suffering.

Ask yourself these three simple questions;

What's bothering you?

What's actually bothering you?

No, what 's *really* bothering you?

2. Accept

Our natural instinct is to push away the feeling of suffering. We think whatever happened *shouldn't* have happened. However, this time ask yourself:

What if it *should* have happened just the way it did?

What if that bad experience taught you something?

What if that hard time guided you (or is guiding you) towards a better path?

What if everything happened just the way it should?

Sit with this for 5 minutes.

3. Move On

This is the exciting part. You can now begin to focus your energy towards creating a future of calm and comfort. Begin to visualise all of the ways you can move forward with your life now that you have made peace with your suffering. It's time to Move On. What are you going to do with your life now?

NOTES TO SELF:

1. Read up on a world religion that you have always wondered about.
2. Fall in love with wisdom.
3. Don't obsess over your problems
4. Listen to a Beyoncé album.
5. Sign up for a class in Tai Chi.

Chapter 5

A Tale of Thanksgiving

Do you remember when you were a child and you were taught to say *Thank You?* Your parents may have sometimes treated it like your entire life depended on getting into the habit of saying this little phrase?

Well it turns out that they were setting you up with one of life's biggest lessons. It wasn't just for the sake of having good manners or being polite, although those things are important, but it turns out that showing a little daily gratitude goes a lot further than you may think.

Okay I know you're probably thinking that writing a chapter on gratitude is a 90's throwback and a self-help cliché – I do agree. But some things, I guess, are timeless and having a sense of appreciation is one of those things.

Let's just do a quick calculation to get your mind ready for the mental gymnastics coming up. There are 168 hours in a week, of which you probably spend 50 to 60 of them sleeping, and about 40 to 50 hours working and commuting. Then you'll spend about 6 hours preparing and eating food and another two and a half hours showering, fixing your hair (and berating yourself in the mirror).

Why's that important?

Because study after study has shown that just 5 minutes a day spent in gratitude will completely change your life. That's 0.49% of your week that will have a tremendous impact on the other 99.51%.

Suddenly gratitude doesn't sound so cliché, right?

Let's explore it further.

***

It seems to be that what the world wants from us is for us to *keep wanting*. When I think back to the times that I was most depressed, it baffles me how I thought that a pair of designer jeans or a new gadget was going to make me happy.

One way I know this manifests for most of us – and especially me - is having a wardrobe filled to the brim with clothes and feeling like you have nothing to wear.

Sound familiar?

This isn't always a new *thing* but can also manifest as wanting more and more of what you might already have a lot of, such as "likes" on Facebook, a better job, more recognition, and some more of those damn qualifications. Maybe you don't have time to sit around and take stock of what you have, because there is really so much more that you want?

Herein lies the lack trap and it's totally *killing your vibe.*

I hate to be the one who has to break it to you but the damn awful truth is that lack will never end.

Nope.

Lack in our lives is a relentless, persistent, tenacious truth and it states that there will always be something you don't have that you want.

Every time. Guaranteed. Next Monday? *Yup.* Next Week? *Absolutely.* This time next year? *For sure.* Even after that big promotion? *Oh yes!*

It's how the world works. We're born, we strive, we accumulate, some succeed, and others don't succeed quite as much. What the world tells us is that if we don't succeed then we are destined to be miserable and the only way to feel fulfilment in life is to acquire all the things we want and do all the things we wish to do.

However, what if there was another way?

What if you could feel that sense of gratitude in your life in spite of what was going on? What if you had the skill of always staying a little optimistic?

I have lots of gratitude stories to choose from, like I said it's a self-help cliché but the best story I can share with you is one that takes place on one of the most grateful days of all...*Thanksgiving.*

THANKSGIVING IN HONG KONG

OK, time for another confession.

Before I tell a story of my experience with gratitude I have to be honest with you and tell you a story of my experience of being unappreciative.

You see, I've been painting a magical and mystical picture of my trip but the truth is that my time in Hong Kong was not all beach walks, Tai Chi, and dancing on rooftops with friends. It was damn hard work quite a bit of the time. My work schedule was demanding, the constant crowds of people were overwhelming, and the humidity was intense enough to sometimes bring a tear to my eye. Figuring out the public transportation was difficult and sometimes scary because one wrong bus ride and I could end up on a deserted road with only Chinese signs and not an English-speaking ear to help.

Simple tasks like using my mobile phone were complicated by having to constantly buy phone credits and load them onto my phone following a Cantonese speaking automated system. My sleep was completely out of sync and I was somehow surviving on about three hours of sleep per night. The tiny "kitchen" (and I uses quotes because it was actually a cupboard of 2 square feet) made it very difficult to prepare any food and I had lost all sense of a regular routine.

However, this is what I had wanted. To be thrown off balance by my life so I could get a sense of what was really important. I had to accept that the reason I may have had so much time to feel the blues was because everything else was just so convenient for me.

I don't say all this to complain, but just to point out that living abroad very often comes with a long line of challenges. After only a few days, I found that the adjustment to living in a foreign country was getting the better of me. So much so that one day when my laptop broke and I had to navigate my way though the extremely busy district of Causeway Bay (kind of like the Times Square of Hong Kong) to track down one of only two Mac repair stores in the city, I got so lost trying to follow the Cantonese signs, that I almost hailed a cab to the airport and went back to England.

I guess I have a flair for the dramatic.

I had to wonder if my default setting at this time was to be a little ungrateful

***

Thanksgiving came around in Hong Kong. Well Canadian Thanksgiving anyway, which is like the American version only celebrated a month earlier. Either way, being British, it wasn't a holiday that I usually had the pleasure of celebrating so I was excited. I'd made some Canadian friends while in Hong Kong and I was thrilled when they invited me to celebrate this holiday with them.

After all, it seemed like the ultimate celebration of gratitude and I was ready to be a student of such a powerful art form.

Also the Pumpkin Pie. Don't forget the Pumpkin Pie!

Enter *Moose* – or so I called her. She was fast becoming one of my closet allies on my Eastern excursion, a young woman from the province of Ontario in Canada, very slim with long gorgeous brown curly hair. She spoke fluent French and English and was so proud of her Canadian heritage that she sported the Maple Leaf on her satchel.

I met Moose in a somewhat tacky club in Hong Kong's infamous party district – the kind of place you only go when you're new in town and you don't know you're getting ripped off by being charged five pounds for a glass of Coke. Somewhere in between the blaring music of *Dancing Queen* and *Single Ladies,* we exchanged numbers and she offered to show me the ropes of the city.

She knew how to find some of the cheapest and the most well hidden restaurants and introduced me to a few locals. I found out that this was Moose's second time living in Hong Kong. She had spent one semester of her undergraduate degree there and fell in love with the city so much so that she had always planned on returning one day. She loved Hong Kong so much I sometimes found it hard to keep up with her enthusiasm.

A Tale of Thanksgiving

"Happy Thanksgiving!" rang out as a crowd of Moose's Canadian friends shouted out to us and we were welcomed into their gorgeous apartment located in the Hong Hom district. The food was cooking, the production line of people was in place, and we all finished drawing around the fingers of our hands to make turkey decorations for the table just in time for Thanksgiving dinner to be served.

After we all destroyed the greatest display of food I had yet come upon in Hong Kong, that moment came where we went around the room to share what we were thankful for. I'd seen this done in movies and always thought it was a beautiful custom. The usual heartfelt answers came up: thankful for family, for friends, for travel, for adventure, for love, for fun, for joy, and for each other. Being part of this tradition and being invited to share it with such wonderful people was not something I would ever take lightly. In fact, in that moment I felt really damn lucky.

A few weeks earlier, I had spoken with one of my friends back at home. She tried to get me to come home when I dared mention how hard I was finding the heat, the crowds, and the numerous complications. She was biased of course and had her own agenda for trying to lure me back home but she did pose a question to me, which I was grateful for. It was a simple question but it had become a tipping point in my journey.

Her question came out as I continued to bitch to her about how hot it was, how I didn't like the food, and how homesick I felt. She stopped me in my tracks and asked me: *When you come through this will you be different? Or will you be the same?*

Whoa. What a profound question, I thought. And even more profound was that the answer was blatantly obvious – *Yes. I would be changed. I expected to be changed.* Isn't that what I wanted more than anything, for my life to transform and improve? Granted, I didn't know *how* I was going to be changed, but even the smallest change was going to make a huge difference.

That discussion with my friend from back home may have been just another conversation for her but it's one I'll always remember because it pushed me to assess my entire

approach to this whole adventure. The journey to _
point might not have been a smooth ride, but who ever said
that change was smooth? Why did I believe that transition,
even to somewhere better, was going to be completely
comfortable? I was beginning to accept that change causes
us to grow, and that personal growth can be chaotic in and
of itself.

So as I shared this story with my friends around the
Thanksgiving table I declared that I was most thankful
for *my chance and ability to embrace change.*

Change is something we can have a hard time dealing
with and our inability to flow with it is what makes so-
called *control freaks* out of many of us. However, if we
scratch below the surface we will probably find that change
is not what we are most frightened of - but instead, we are
terrified that things may *not* change.

I looked around the table and felt a little more peace in
my soul; in fact, it had just barged its way in.

WHAT WE PLAN VS WHAT ACTUALLY HAPPENS

I love following TV shows.

Getting involved in a good series and watching episode after episode is probably my favourite way to chill out.

There are a few legal dramas on my list that I would never miss because they're written in such a way that you get to see inside of somebody's soul when they are on the stand in court. I saw an episode once where a three-way couple were asking the court to be legally allowed a three-way marriage. It was two women and a man. The lawyer who was cross-examining one of the women asked her a pointed and personal question - "Is this how you thought your life would work out? A three-way-marriage?"

The woman calmly and eloquently responded by saying, "No, my life didn't work out the way I had planned, but you know what? It did work out."

Don't worry if you don't get the point yet.

Just contemplate that for a while.

The meaning I found in this example and her comment is that very often what happens in our life is actually far more interesting and exciting than what we wish would have happened in the first place. So often, we have a story running through our head about all the things that we're not satisfied about; the things that haven't happened, the things we want, the things we were disappointed by, and the jealously we might feel when you see that somebody else has what you want.

This is how I lived my life but I had to learn to become grateful for the inevitable truth that my life was always moving forward and working out. I had to stop missing out on all the fun I was having hoping for all of the fun I *hoped* I'd be having.

The Universe has a plan that works. *We don't.* The more we accept this as fact, the happier we become. I've learned that when we fully accept that things maybe won't all go the way we've planned, then we can start to enjoy the bends and curves of our real life much more often.

I wondered if it was just me who viewed life this way, so I asked a number of successful adults this question: *Did your life work out the way you expected?*

Here are just a few of the responses I got:

"I planned to study medicine at University but after I was rejected instead I took a year to travel and earn some money. I made some of the best friends I could imagine."

"I planned to move to New York City but after things didn't work out there, I moved back home to my parents. It was horrible at first but it gave me the time to focus on growing my own business. Now I work for myself and travel to New York frequently on vacation."

"I planned on finishing my Ph.D. in three years, but after a long series of re-writes, it took me almost six years. But you know what? In those extra years, I was invited to speak at a prestigious conference where I then got a published article. That was what ultimately kicked off my career."

The statements above are from people who really had moments when they thought their lives were completely off track. The ego mind told them that they were failing, stalling and regressing. However, in actually fact, life was showing them a better way.

That's something I've come to learn and love about life; it has a tendency to know the way even when we have no idea.

All you have to do is follow the inescapable path life will lay down before you and enjoy the view from where you are.

THE DOWNWARD COMPARISON TRICK

It's hard to deny that we are creatures of upward-social-comparison. It's natural to us. Anybody who has ever heard of the phrase *keeping up with the Joneses* will know this is true and I've spoken a bit about it already.

What we're actually doing is striving to be a more improved version of ourselves and make our status concern our sole purpose for living.

It used to be that we just looked at our peers for a benchmark to compare ourselves too and then along came social media, a place where we can all go to feel a little inferior. Pop culture cranked it up a notch by putting countless Reality Shows on TV showing the lives of those who seem to have a far more glamorous deal than us.

Don't get me wrong. I love social media and I certainly keep up with the Kardashian's but I have been guilty of becoming overly concerned about my profile and my social standing. I believe that reality shows and social media should come with a warning label that reads – *"Beware. Proceed with caution. Overly long sessions of comparing yourself with other people will cause depression, anxiety and panic."*

But what if you could turn your natural instinct for social comparison on its head and use it to bring you a greater sense of peace?

Well I believe that you can.

In his world-famous book *The Art of Happiness*, The Dalai Lama talks about happiness being achieved through being thankful for what *we don't have.*

This may sound counter intuitive but this little technique has become one of the best principles for peace that I have ever found. Now that I have been practicing gratitude, I am also so much easier on *myself.*

When I read about the Dalai Lama, his materials referenced research that shows that people will always remain unhappy while comparing themselves to the rich and famous people in this world. If you focus only on the toned and beautiful people at the gym for example, and the thriving and flourishing career people on the front of Forbes magazine, of course, you're going to feel down. But what if you instead compared your life to that of an inmate in the county jail or someone struggling for years to find any kind of job? It's certain that you will gain a greater and more realistic viewpoint of your world.

So what advice can I offer here?

Look around.

Drink it all in.

Notice how many wonderful and beautiful things are around you.

Feel grateful.

And then move on with your day.

Still Hunting For Happiness

Considering I had clearly had a strong hit of the powerful ways gratitude could change my DNA (well, that's what it felt like), I began to wonder if gratitude was so powerful, could it bring me lasting happiness?

Here I was in Hong Kong on the hunt for happiness, thinking that it was all about *Me, Me, Me.* That's sometimes the spiritual trap; you become increasingly and unhealthily focused on your own thoughts, feelings and mood and you forget that the most spiritual thing you can do is to chill out every now and again.

After all I was in one of the most exciting cities in the world, one that offered gusto, adventure, exquisite dining, and pristine white beaches, but I had been so busy focusing on finding inner peace that I had neglected to sample the famous egg tarts or enjoy the nightly symphony of lights on Kowloon Pier on a regular basis. Thus I officially declared that it was time to not take myself so seriously. I allowed myself to temporarily get off my where-is-my-life-going-next merry-go-round and go in search of a different kind of contentment; the type that can be found at a glittery rooftop cocktail bar named *Sugar*.

This place was so extravagant that the bathroom appeared to be made of pure crystal. Not only did this pink neon hideout make the best pina coladas in town, it also offered the best views for miles.

My friends and I enjoyed a Saturday night of bliss looking out over the city that was quickly becoming our new home. Luxurious bamboo loungers decorated the shiny marble terrace and we slouched back on these chairs full of our own self-importance and enjoyed the convenience of table service for all of our cocktail needs. Despite my spiritual philosophy and recent brushes with divinity, I didn't abstain from alcohol. One of life's pleasures when out with friends.

So there we were staring out at more than 6,000 skyscrapers, all of which were taking part in a light show filling the city with bright green lasers, hot pink floodlights, and red illuminations. I was being gently kissed by the warm night breeze, it was clear that I had found my own little piece of heaven on this rooftop. But no sooner had I inhaled the pleasure, all of a sudden I began to contemplate my life once again, and I asked my friends, "Do you think we'll ever be happy?"

"What?" Sophia replied in shock. My question came pretty much out of the blue. "Are you not happy?" Moose chimed in, with a worried tone in her voice.

Well, that was an interesting question. *Was I happy?* Sure it felt great to carelessly wander around the city, but *inner and enduring happiness?* The jury was still out.

"I mean, here we are in a breath-taking city, not a care in the world, in great company, and yet I'm sure we'll still find something to bitch about," I said. There was a collective giggle and a unanimous consensus.

"Maybe we will never be happy?" Moose added.

What a horrible thought! But what if she was right? I'd gone on a quest for happiness quite a few times in my life and was left with the same feeling of dissatisfaction. I hunted happiness down in the form of my college degree. I pursued peace in every romantic relationship I embarked on. I even chased contentment all the way to California and back, but everywhere I went and every enlightenment expedition I went on, happiness still seemed elusive.

"Well, maybe happiness is not something we get to keep," Moose added thoughtfully, and I liked where she was going with that. She went on, "I mean, we feel happy sometimes and we don't other times. There are times when we laugh and other times we don't. So whenever we do have something to enjoy, we should be extra grateful for it because it won't last forever. Like everything, it will eventually come to an end."

And just like that, I felt she had hit the nail on the head. I let go of my need to be entirely happy all the time I realised that sometimes I would be happy and other times I wouldn't. However, one thing was for sure, the less I harassed myself to go in search of it more often than not it came and found me.

And just like I leaned into my life a little more, content with the fact that I would not always be happy but confident that I can take the time to enjoy it when I was.

We drank our cocktails.

We jumped on the tram and travelled around the city.

We ate fast food at 2am.

And Lori and I raced home through the wonderful district of Sheung Wan.

Yes, I was happy.

NOTES TO SELF:

1. Cook a Thanksgiving style meal and invite friends over.
2. Decide to embrace change.
3. Ration your bitchin'.
4. Help those less fortunate than yourself.
5. Remember that you are not the centre of the universe.

Chapter 6

Learn a Little Sanskrit

In Hong Kong I came across such an array of different religious traditions and spiritual practices. As a former colony of the British Empire, Hong Kong upholds a strong Christian faith while still honouring its Eastern roots. It was common for me to pass a church, a temple, and a mosque while on my way to pick up some milk. It was even more ordinary to pass a Buddhist monk wandering the streets as I passed through the night markets.

My apartment sat next to the famous Man Mo Temple, which I never actually saw *closed*. Anybody at anytime can visit the temple to worship or just look around. Whenever I saw it, I noticed that it looked a bit vulnerable, but unharmed and esteemed. I couldn't help but aspire to be like that temple.

With spirituality in the air everywhere, so much aroused my attention. While other visitors might roam freely around a strange city seeking museums, a Michelin Star restaurant, or a trendy mall, I always seemed to find myself at a meditation group or metaphysical workshop. This would probably explain why I was drawn to *Lata*, an Indian lady who lives in Tsim Sha Tsui who I had met one day at work. She once shared her daily morning ritual with me:

"Every morning, I pray for one hour," she informed me. "And then I meditate for one hour." As much as I was amazed by this discipline, my mind instantly started to the do the math and work out what crazy early time this lady must awaken every morning. *Is it 4 a.m., is it 3 a.m.?* Before I had time to work out this none-of-my-business equation, Lata leaned in and asked me, "So, do you like to meditate?"

I was excited by her question, but I wasn't sure how to answer. After all, I did like to meditate but I was never one to get beyond a ten-minute guided meditation found on YouTube. All I could seem to recall in that moment was the frustrated times I sat cross-legged on my bedroom floor in Liverpool doing whatever I could to shut my mind the hell up.

I'd learned that sometimes it's necessary to share details with somebody and sometimes they are simply looking for a straightforward answer because they simply want to help. I suspected this was one of the latter situations, so I answered, "Yes, I do like to meditate."

"Well that settles it," Lata replied. 'You must come to my meditation centre with me."

LIVING IN FEAR

Let's face it; living in fear is unpleasant. In fact it's downright awful. Fear seems to be the staple diet of anybody smart enough to notice how stressful modern life can be. There are plenty of remedies out there to combat fear; traditional psychological approaches, Reiki Healing, therapy and not to mention the pile of self-help books. All of these techniques have their place and merits for certain people, and I know this because I tried several of them. It seems today that people are running around in fear because they are scared of being in fear; turns out - *nothing to fear but fear itself* - was a pretty spot on statement. However, let's pause for a moment and address fear not as the total senseless creature it is often portrayed to be. There *is* healthy fear; the kind of fear that you would have in a fight or flight response or the nerves you would get before a job interview. Or even the fear you have that nudges you to go to the doctor if you have been feeling sick. This kind of fear helps you focus and is actually a survival mechanism that has been serving you well your entire life. Let's put it this way; if ancient man didn't feel fear and run away from the sabre-toothed tiger then there would be no you or me today. However, here's the difference, once ancient man had run away from the tiger he would find a place to rest and sleep for a good 48 hours. We don't do this. We drink a cup of coffee and *soldier on*. We don't take time to recuperate and before we know it we are in fear of every damn thing; an unpleasant email, a meeting with our boss, public speaking, social outings, being fired, being judged, being criticised or not being enough.

Sound familiar yet?

Well it turns out that I did find a way to slowly but surely combat away at my undertone of terror and that was through the practice of *meditation.*

***

Meditating. I *think* it's a verb. It means to focus one's mind for a period of time. You might think of it as a tool for relaxation, and it goes by other names too, such as mindfulness, guided imagery, or quiet contemplation. Whatever you call it, there are any number of studies out there that prove that the practice of meditation combats stress, it can help you sleep better, it improves overall health, and it brings down general levels of anxiety and fear.

Whenever anyone asks me about meditation, I sum it up this way. Life wants us to be happy now. Life is not interested in what plans we have to *put off* happiness until some perfect future timeframe. *Nope.* Meditation is something that happens in the here and now, and trains our minds to live more consciously in the here and now.

THE MANY WAYS MEDITATIONS MOVES US

When we meditate, we cooperate with life's wish for us to be happy and clear our mind of any thoughts that try to convince us otherwise. Meditation is the space in which we expose the nonsense our mind has been telling us and open ourselves up to a new way of thinking.

So what does meditation look like? You might have an image in your mind of somebody sitting cross-legged on the floor, burning incense, and chanting, "Ommmmmm." I've tried it that way and it's really moving, rather traditional, but if you're just getting started, then your first practice of meditation doesn't have to involve such a rigid regime.

The great news is that you can meditate in an endless number of ways. You can close your eyes or leave them open. You can stand up, sit down, or walk gently through nature. You can do it remaining still in a silent room or on the way to work. *The only key ingredient necessary for successful meditation is the willingness to go inside of yourself … no matter how uncomfortable that may be.*

LEARNING TO SLOW DOWN

Within a week or so, I found myself standing outside the Tin Hau Metro station as I anxiously wait for Lata to emerge from the bright orange underground and walk me to my first ever formal meditation. The meditation centre we visited taught a very specific meditation practice known as *Raja Yoga,* or more traditionally *Aṣṭāng,* and I learned that I was expected to undergo eight weeks of tuition in the practice.

I had been assigned to a tutor named Anika, a middle-aged Malaysian lady who really seemed to know her stuff. "So, why would you like to start meditation?" Anika lovingly asked me as she sipped her cup of warm water with lemon. My answer was simple: "To quiet my mind."

"And why would you want to do that?" Anika giggled. I was a little taken aback because I thought I had given the standard answer. *Isn't quieting my mind what meditation is about?* Anika must have seen the confused look on my face and saved me by interrupting my thinking.

"Meditation is not about emptying your mind. It is about filling your mind with the right things," she patiently explained. This was a new concept to me and remaining in my role of student I curiously asked "such as?"

"The original qualities of the soul. *Peace, Love, and Bliss.*"

Let's pause here.

So the original qualities of the soul – as I was being taught – are: *Peace, Love, and Bliss.* Okay, I think I got it. "So, *I am* peace, love and bliss?" I asked her to make sure I understood.

"There is so much peace, love, and bliss in you that if you could focus on that in your mind, you would be startled at how happy you could be … so stop living in so much fear," Anika replied.

There is again; that word *fear.* I didn't feel fearful in any way at Anika's words but I was definitely familiar with the concept she was conveying to me. I leaned into the conversation a little more and decided not to shy away from my own fear.

At this point of my journey, I was definitely becoming a more confident spiritual seeker. I was meditating, learning Buddhist philosophy, and being one of those people who counted their blessings. But I was by no means about to wear an orange robe, shave my head and retire to a mountain in India.

Here's the thing. When it came to being a "spiritual" person, I'm pretty sure that I didn't check all the boxes. I didn't have any psychic gifts. I didn't burn incense. I still really loved to drink coffee, indulge in celebrity culture and make Friday night plans. This didn't make me a bad person, but just another spiritual seeker in a modern world, just like you, learning to balance both my spiritual side and my human side, carrying a yoga mat in one hand and a vanilla latte in the other.

What I learned from Anika and from Tai Chi and from the many teachers in my travels is that we actually don't have to choose between our human side and our spiritual side; we just have to choose between joy and misery. I hope you get the same sense of relief I did to find out that being down-to-earth can still make you a really good candidate to teach the world how to be that little bit happier.

OM SHANTI

There is a phrase in Sanskrit which I had become well acquainted with - *Om Shanti.* Sanskrit is the ancient language of India and the language of Hindu and Buddhist worship. This phrase, *Om Shanti,* was used for many purposes at the centre. I heard it exchanged when I saw people greeting, thanking or welcoming one another. And when I saw Anika receive a gift from her fellow *Yoga Sister* - all of the teachers refer to each other and sisters and brothers - I heard the expression used yet again ... *Om Shanti.*

This phrase is made up from the perfect marrying of both Sanskrit and Hindi forms of expression. They explained to me that the English translation is: *I am peace.*

These three syllables created a sound so beautiful that it awakened something within me that has been sleeping for years. So I began to play around with this phrase because it was just so beautiful. Even years later, I'm still learning my way around it as if beginning to play the piano and needing to explore every key.

Join me and allow this beautiful sound to dance gently on your tongue. Slowly, slowly. Feel how it sounds on your tongue. *Om ... Shan ... Tee.* And again, *Om ... Shan ... Tee.* And again, *Om ... Shan ... Tee.*

I am peace.

You are peace.

We are peace.

It didn't matter how I said it and I wasn't sure the English translation was even all that relevant. All I knew was that these words echoed an ancient truth that my soul seemed to have known for all eternity, something it had been trying to tell me every time I took to my bed in another session of self-loathing or chose to hang out with jealousy or judgement instead of extending peace. *I am peace, I am peace, I am peace.*

Everything else I have added onto myself seemed useless in comparison. All of my own self-important characteristics merely buried the universal truth that I was peace, love and bliss. Somewhere underneath all of my own crap lay something humble and self-assured.

The only time I fall away from my truth is in any moment I don't believe this is real. Sure, I may know it for the rest of my life and it will always be a nice idea, but it is only when I believe it fully, when I am*convinced* of this statement more so than I am convinced that the grass is green, that I enter into the space that The Universe is holding for me.

I felt comfortable at the time, and I still do, that there is no rush to claim this special place held specifically for me by The Universe. My name is on it. Besides, nobody else is going to claim my spot because they don't need to – *everyone has their own.*

All along I had thought I was alone in my search for peace. Little did I know that *peace* was also looking for me, that it had a function I could fulfil for it. The only question left was -*was I going to be who I'd always been or step into becoming somebody new?*

Again, sometimes this stuff got a bit heavy, I'll admit it. But it's kind of impossible to learn to quiet your mind unless you're willing to allow your brain to be scrambled just a little. My brain was doing cross-country running on this subject for years. I had been walking around my entire life attached to anger, guilt and resentment without taking even one minute to contemplate that I was actually *Love, Peace, and Bliss.*

HOW TO MEDITATE

Anika had taught me a lot during the eight weeks. I learned that there was endless love, peace and bliss inside of me and that I was keeping it away by living in fear. We talked about the ego – and how when we identify with our achievements and success too much then we won't be able to find happiness, just more fear.

I also learned that my mind was like a giant traffic jam with thousands of thoughts wanting to be heard. That I knew. I heard that screeching inside my head from before. But now there was something I could do to stop it. The answer was to enter into a meditation practice and do it every day.

I remember the day the general lesson was over and the time had come for me to put my knowledge to work and join the group off in the adjoining room of the Raja Yoga Centre. The room itself was not what I had expected. It was like a living room you'd find in most suburban homes. The lighting was very dim. Beige carpets, beige walls, two white sofas, and a collection of meditation cushions all facing towards the front wall where a small light, no bigger than the size of a fairy light, poked through the wall and became the main focus of the entire room.

Anika told me that this light was what I must look at when I meditated. I am allowed (and obligated) to keep my eyes open while I did so. "This is so our minds stay focused," Anika told me. "When we close our eyes, our thoughts swing from one tree to another."

We took our seats amid the group and both sat comfortably on the white sofa at the back of the room. We looked at the small light and some relaxing music began to play in the background. *3 ... 2 ... 1... Meditate.*

THE OPEN EYES MEDITATION PRACTICE

I'm not a person who likes to make meditation complicated. Life is complicated enough. The art of sitting and being still is as simple as it seems on the outside. There isn't really a lot of rules and you should do what is most comfortable for you. It works because your part is very minimal and The Universe's part is huge.

So at this point, I would like to invite you to try this very powerful form of meditation. All you'll need to do is find a comfortable place to sit. You don't need to cross your legs or make any symbols with your fingers or hands. Just relax completely.

For the first step, I was told it was helpful to make a request before you begin meditation that goes like this. *Dear Mind: I am about to enter into meditation. I thank you for being concerned about my well-being and how you look for various solutions to my problems, however I am now giving you some time off and something else is going to take over. I assure you that I will come back to you in a short time and ask that for the time being, you do not interrupt. Thank You.*

In this meditation practice, don't close your eyes. Keep them open and focused on a certain spot in the room. If you'd like then light a candle and have this be your point of focus. Play some calming music or a mantra in the background. Or repeat to yourself the mantra I introduced earlier: Om Shanti.

You only have one job for the next 5 minutes. Focus on the point of light and remember that at your core, you are love, peace and joy. This is the only truth you need to remember for the next 5 minutes. As you practice, you can increase the time, but start out with 5 minutes and gain confidence (and peace) as you go.

After your meditation, you can close with a second request by stating something like this: *Dear Universe, May I remain in this state when faced with the challenges of the day. I make a conscious effort to lock in the energy of this meditation and allow the peace within me to spill into my day. Thank you.*

RELEASING AND SOLVING PROBLEMS

Once you begin to feel comfortable with meditation as a daily practice, you can use it to improve your life in hundreds of ways. I'm going to talk about a few here, and there are more ideas that you can access through my website.

One of the first variations that I found tremendously liberating was to use meditation to release and solve problems in my life. The process of release is about giving away your problems to The Universe with the clear intent and expectation that the right solutions will come to your attention.

Contrast this to the old way of thinking. You might have been taught that the way to solve something was to relentlessly hold on to it, like a dog with a bone, and analyse it to death until you figured out a solution. I believed this for years too and I became very good at obsessing about my problems, I can tell you.

But from a spiritual perspective, the opposite is true. In order to solve a problem in our lives, it is actually better to release it from our minds so that the most powerful solution can come forward. The Universe will acknowledge every conscious decision we make to release our worries, and will act on our behalf to bring us to a greater sense of peace about anything that upsets us, including some of our biggest and most complex problems.

The most effective way to hand over your problems to The Universe is with a repetitive instruction to your mind.

I learned this is a rather simple four-step process and I have been amazed at how well it works.

Step One: Identify your problem.

Step Two: Decide to release it.

Step Three: Believe that it is being taken care of.

Step Four: Return to your daily activities as normal.

Let me explain how it works with a real life example.

Step One and Step Two: stating the problem and releasing it: *Dear Universe, I am having a problem with jealously. I release this to you and trust that you can deal with this better than I can. Thank You.*

Step Three: believe it is being taken care of.

Step Four: just return to your daily activities.

The Universe is working behind the scenes and nudging you toward a better approach to your problem.

As new thoughts come into your mind or you notice that somebody points you in the direction of a relevant article– know that this is The Universe guiding you. Sometimes the guidance is to do nothing. Either way, listen and trust yourself.

The more you test this approach the more confident you will become in your ability to solve your problems. The quietness of your meditation practice opens up your mind. As you begin to trust that all things are happening in your life as they are supposed to be, this naturally helps to lower your levels of fear and anxiety. Remember, you are *Love, Peace, and Bliss and everything happens right on time.*

FINDING YOUR TRUTH

I have discovered and accepted that there are two aspects to the truth: *telling the truth* and *listening to the truth.* We often go to great lengths to convince ourselves of our limitations (untruths) and sometimes even go to great lengths to convince others of theirs. You don't need to continue to live this way. Instead, I am suggesting that you use meditation to find your truth and keep yourself spiritually awake. This can be done in a number of ways. I'm going to suggest four techniques here but I bet you can imagine many more ways that truth can be used to improve your life.

First, tell yourself the truth. Make a daily habit to remind yourself of your original qualities and you'll find this is a sure way to keep yourself spiritually awake. In the shower, in the car, and at your computer, whatever you are doing, just keep reminding yourself of the truth within you by affirming, "I am Love, Peace and Bliss.

Second, tell somebody else the truth. Judging another person is a sure sign that you have fallen asleep and forgotten your own truth. By acknowledging another's true qualities, you will instantly awaken. This can be done by checking your thoughts.

Third, tell the truth about your boundaries. There is nothing spiritual about being walked all over. Even though your intentions may be kind hearted, it's important to inform the people around you of where your boundaries lie.

Fourth, be willing to see the truth. We are so often reluctant to receive a compliment. When someone says something nice to us, we may feel shy, vulnerable, and on some level, *undeserving.* Once you have committed to staying spiritually awake, it is vital that you graciously receive compliments, blessings, and acts of kindness. You do deserve them because you are indeed a good person. Remember, you are *Peace, Love, and Bliss.*

USING QUICK MEDITATION POINTS DURING THE DAY

In spite of your best efforts, your thoughts can start to race out of control at any point in your day, sometimes without warning. I have tried the following technique to try to stop this train wreck in my mind. I call it a form of *traffic control* for our minds.

Take just a short 60 seconds at a few points during the day to sit in silence and become open to The Universe's message for you at that time. Allow yourself to sink into a place of pure openness for the next 60 seconds. Don't worry if you think that your request has not been answered in that minute of silence. Trust that you will get an answer throughout the course of the day.

Another quick point of meditation that is very effective is at the end of the day. I believe that we close our day with the same care in which we opened it, so that as we sleep, we can release all resistance. When we sleep it is a fantastic chance for The Universe to work on us without our damn interference.

To do this, allow yourself to ease into a quiet space in your mind. Allow yourself to drifting beyond all your experiences, worries and excitements from the day.

Softly affirm: *Dear Universe: Today is drawing to an end. Thank you for all the ways in which I got it right.*

COMMIT TO THE MEDITATION MONTH

Meditation becomes as much of a habit as anything else that we include in our morning, evening and daily routine. The same way we never fail to get out of bed, comb our hair, choose our clothes, or lock our front door, we can learn to ensure that before leaving our homes, we check in with The Universe.

Meditation has the capacity to transform your life, but just like going to the gym, if you don't put in the work, you will not get the results. To ensure that meditation becomes a non-negotiable daily ritual in your life, first make a habit out of it. The formula is simple: *Daily Meditation for One Month Equals Transformation, even if it's small.*

Once you make a habit out of it you will start to feel the benefits.

STANDING IN THE RAIN.

I've often stood in the rain. In England it's a sure deal that a few hundred times a year you are going to be expected to unwillingly get caught in the rain, however, now November had arrived in Hong Kong and I was surprised to discover that my relationship with this force of nature had followed me – In the middle of my Asian hide-out the skies had finally broken (and not just for short burst of storm-type rain but for a lengthy period of wet and cold days).

I guess a lot of me was a little relived to finally be subject to cooler weather, I could finally wear my jeans again and become reacquainted with a green American Apparel hoodie that I loved so much.

In many ways this rain perfectly merged home with Hong Kong and this merging actually couldn't have come at a more appropriate time. I am expecting a visitor from home, my friend Ling who I used to work with back in

Liverpool. I hadn't known Ling for long, she was somebody who had come into my life only shortly before I left Liverpool and commenced on my Asian adventure. We had remained in touch and since she was coming to Asia to visit her family in Beijing she has arranged to come via Hong Kong and spend four days with me.

We had booked into a hotel in the Fortress Hill district and don't seem to be able to enjoy the benefits of the outdoor pool, rooftop or balconies because of the rain. She is disappointed with the weather.

None-the-less once we see our deluxe hotel room and more notably our glass-walled bathroom with a hot tub the size of a small pool our mood remarkably lifted. Ling and I find sanctuary in this hot tub as we meet there for nightly *put-the-world-to-rights* conversations.

'Do you miss home?' Ling asked me.

'I really do', I reply, sinking into a nostalgic slump.

'When do you think you'll come home? How long are you gonna stay here for?'

'I still don't know, my journey definitely isn't over yet'

'What do you think you'll do when you get home?',
Ling asked.

Now this was a question everybody traveling hates.

In fact this is a question that anybody hates. Always
being asked what you are going to do *next*.

This question always has a way of depleting what you're
currently doing and makes it not enough in your own head.
It's not hard to look around at the world, especially in a
busy city, and notice that everybody is more concerned
with what they are about to do next than what they are
doing now. And there I was slipping into my own
existential crisis again. A familiar, yet boring place.

My negativity began to make me feel heavy. The toxins
of my self-disapproval were impacting on my body and
oozing from my pores – as I had just been on a crazy
drinking binge and the hangover was setting in.

***

Ling and I filled out time in Hong Kong with the
perfect fuse of touristy hotspots and local hangouts; we

both knew the city somewhat well by now and could recommend a few places to each other.

I drank potato milk, as recommended by my friend and visited the large Jackie Chan statue on the Kowloon Pier.

However, just a few days later the time had come for my friend to continue on her journey to main land China and for me to return to my regular life in Hong Kong. I say my goodbyes to Jing on the underground train and in true dramatic style; watching the train pull away as her body became a blur in the fast moving carriage.

Her question still bothered me; what was I going to do *next?*

Though it was romantic to flee my life and gallivant around Hong Kong my thoughts began to ask what was I *really* going to do.

Once again, I was finding myself with the burden of not enough.

I emerged to ground level where the persistent downpour of rain greeted me and, to say the least, I was feeling emotional.

I was existentially exhausted. I had no choice but to bring all of my shame to the table and simply stand in the rain. In that moment I began to claim the healing I had been experiencing at Raja Yoga and allowed the rain to wash away my stains of sadness. So, there in the rain, I took a seat and began to meditate the best way I knew how.

I kept my eyes open.

I allowed the world to continue going by.

I remembered that peace was within me, somewhere underneath all of my own crap.

The raindrops fall in such heavy splashes that for all I know I'm crying but I can't tell.

Meditation is kind of like the rain.

If you stand in it long enough it starts to wash things away.

So, I just sat there and allowed anything that was not authentically me to wash away.

Notes to Self:

1. Meditate every day. No exception. Just do it. If only just for 5 minutes.

2. Don't be scared to get a little spiritual.

3. Read a book by a famous Yogi.

4. Visit a meditation centre or take a meditation class.

5. Remember that meditation is like the rain eventually it washes everything away.

Chapter 7

Connect with Something, Somewhere, Somehow

This is the point where I bring up the word we are all a little afraid to say. Before I do, let me tell you a quick story about when I was a young Catholic boy living in Ireland.

You see, when I was growing up, I used to pray a lot throughout my day. I would say prayers in the morning, prayers at school, prayers before food, and prayers before bedtime. Then on Sunday I would go to the church and pray some more.

I didn't really know what I was doing. I just prayed because I was told I *should*. I also only said the words that I was told to say, which in my case was the Our Father and the Hail Mary.

Then I turned thirteen. I began to form my own thoughts and theories about religion and I rebelled against my Catholic upbringing. I decided that I was through with all of that. Nevertheless, there was one part of upbringing that I couldn't shake and that was the belief that something, somewhere, somehow was bigger and more powerful than me.

So if I may, I'd like to talk about that something, somewhere, somehow that is most commonly known as *God*. You can call this concept whatever word that works for you; for some of you I know this might be an uncomfortable topic but stay with me.

YOU CAN CALL IT WHATEVER YOU LIKE

First let me point out the common trap here. I know the minute I bring up the word *God* you may bring to mind the traditional biblical image of an almighty and powerful God. An authoritarian old man in the sky, quick to anger and ready to judge you for being good or bad.

But this is not the kind of God I'm talking about. What I'm speaking about is that wondrous, mystical, iconic force that nobody really seems to be able to put their hands on. Yet this concept is something that we as humans try to understand throughout our lives.

If it helps you, as it has often helped me, you can call this concept or this entity something different. Personally, I like to call it The Universe.

Really there are many lovely names for it: Love, The Divine, Grace, the list goes on but for simplicity here I will use the fitting word *The Universe* and trust that you know I am talking about the God of your own choosing.

For me, when I say *The Universe* I'm simply talking about that *something somewhere somehow* bigger thing than me.

What I care about is finding a way for you to connect with it as opposed to looking for a word we can all agree on.

You might wonder, if this is such a touchy subject, why bother talking about it at all? Because it's interesting and intriguing? Because after thousands of years of contemplation, you feel like you may be the one to crack the code? *No.* It's because connecting with that *something somewhere somehow* will have a radical impact on how you live your life.

I won't ask if you believe in *The Universe* as a cosmic force that can intervene in your life, but rather I'd like to know: *Do you believe that everything that happens is a mere fluke?*

My answer to this question is *No.* I don't believe that everything that happens is a fluke. I'll explain my reasoning in this chapter, but for now I'd like you to know that it is my sincere desire that by the end of this book you may find a better appreciation for your own version of that *something somewhere somehow.*

MEETING THE UNIVERSE AT THE MOSQUE

If you turn left out of Exit A in the Tsim Tsa Tsui district of Hong Kong you would see the Kowloon Mosque. You could hardly miss it. It's huge and picturesque. Tourists stand for hours taking pictures of its beauty and its complete dominance in the district makes it impossible to ignore.

I really wanted to go in but as someone not of the Islamic faith I was unsure that I would be allowed to enter. One day, my curiosity overtook my fear and I walked up to the front doors of the mosque.

Wow. The building inside was exquisite, grandiose and vast. I had to pass through tall metal gates and climb a striking stone staircase just to get up close. I removed my shoes, washed my feet, and followed all other instructions I had been given so I could enter.

Contrary to being hustled away, I found myself being warmly welcomed by the members of the Mosque who were preparing for their third formal prayer of the day. I would come to learn that every mosque has a *mihrab*, a sconce on the wall that points in the direction of Mecca, the Islamic city of pilgrimage. The importance of Mecca to Muslims is incalculable. This *mirhrab* signifies the direction towards which Muslims pray.

I was politely chaperoned to a prayer bench at the back of the main male prayer room on the second floor. Without sounding cliché, there was definitely a *feeling* in the air. I was in apprehension about experiencing this thing called *God, The Universe, Love and Grace.* In keeping with my inclusive view of The Universe, I removed any traditional connotations about God, Allah or Mohamed, and I just allowed myself to await the arrival of the *something, somewhere, somehow.*

I watched respectfully as more than 100 men gathered in the ritual of Muslim prayer. To me, it was the perfect combination of movement, grace, devotion and song, and it hypnotically absorbed me into its magic and I wondered when or if I would feel any difference in the presence of something bigger than myself.

I watched as they first stood and prayed. They bowed, kneeled and touched their forehead to the floor. It was graceful and beautiful to see them in unison repeating the movements and prayer.

Standing, Bow, Forehead, Kneel, Kneel, Face to the Right, Face to the Left.

These movements are symbolic; combining to form the perfect recipe of intention, openness, devoutness, mercy and glory. Each man looked absorbed by his devotion. I thought to myself, *they are with their everything.* They are giving their *everything.*

It's not a performance to them or a trend they are trying out. This was pure dedication, and to me, I could see their faces were etched with earnest sincerity. *Focused. Fierce. Fixated.* To me, there appeared to be nothing on their mind in this moment but getting closer to that *something, somewhere, somehow.*

FINDING MY OWN CONNECTION.

I felt the emotion and passion at the Mosque. They had clearly found their own God but I still wasn't exactly sure about my own *something, somewhere, somehow* and how I could connect with it? It made me think about the nature of this concept and how it manifests differently for different people.

I believe that if I asked one hundred people passing me on the street if they would like to have a *religious experience,* very few might actually say "yes". However, if I asked them if they'd like to have a *spiritual experience,* my instincts tell me that they would say "absolutely". I trust this is because having a spiritual experience doesn't require following any rules, rituals or rights of passage. It's just a brief moment in time where you see beyond your limited individual self into something *bigger.*

It is my belief that we are having a *spiritual experience* every time we participate in an activity or task that brings us joy. If you want to experience your own feeling of being closer to your *something, somewhere, somehow* then ask yourself this: What am I doing when I am *who I am* without any effort?

I'll give you a moment to ponder this. It's important. *What are you doing when you most feel like your true self without any effort at all?*

My answer is that I feel most myself when I am meditating, in prayer or even listening to Beyoncé (or music in general). I also feel that way when I am writing poetry, painting, or drinking a great cup of coffee.

Notice how hardly any of my *spiritual experiences* require any kind of religious belief at all.

I always ask this question at my workshops and I get so many diverse answers and some common ones. For example, people say they feel this way when they are gardening, reading detective novels, dancing, being with animals, walking in the rain, drawing or sculpting, or just pushing their daughter on a swing.

The possibilities are endless so this is why I say to people to find their own spiritual path rather than adopting the rules and regulations as prescribed by someone else. It is my belief that you have it all figured out on your own.

EXPLORING THIS FURTHER

With each new experience of formal religions that I had not seen before and the many informal spiritual practices, I was gradually learning more about my own *something, somewhere, somehow.* At the meditation centre I attended, Anika had been instructing me in the importance of meditation as an every day practice. She also taught me new chants and encouraged me to read up on spirituality on a daily basis. I had become an active student of a well know metaphysical text called *A Course In Miracles* and was working on its workbook every morning. I felt as if I was a researcher exploring all of the different interpretations of that *something, somewhere, somehow* and seeking a place where it all met in the middle for me.

Along the way, I made a friend in Hong Kong, a wonderful man who owned a new age centre in the central district. I visited him and wondered if I could ask him about his beliefs in something bigger than himself. He obliged.

I sensed a need to get to the point so I started out with the *why* first. So I asked him, "Why bother having a belief in a something bigger than ourselves at all?"

His answer was immediate and life affirming. "Because how awesome is it that there is something amazing and huge out there in The Universe that loves and supports us?" He shared with me that he got extraordinary comfort from even the slightest belief that something else was in play in the world. This made him never feel alone.

His words stuck with me and got me thinking about a word in the religion of Hinduism, *Marga*, which means your 'path'; an individually prescribed route towards your own peace. I love this word because it's inclusive. From what I understand, *Marga* is of one's own choosing, a distinctive and unique path which you choose for yourself on your way to peace. You are not forced to follow a certain set of beliefs in order to reach peace nor is anyone imposing a belief system upon you. This approach simply gives you a nudge and allows you to pave the way for yourself.

The reason why I have grown to enjoy this word, *Marga*, so much is because I love the idea of picking and mixing together diverse religious and spiritual customs and fusing them together into my own personalised practice. I guess it's all part of my *Marga*.

SO, WHAT'S A SPIRITUAL PERSON ANYWAY?

Some of the most lively and impassioned discussions I have with people from around the world is this; *what makes a person spiritual?* Sometimes I will have people ask me how I can consider myself a spiritual seeker and still be going out for drinks and a concert with friends?

Many of us believe that there are a set of rules we must follow in order to 'be spiritual': *we mustn't eat meat; we must only listen to meditation music; we must only drink herbal tea; we must never get angry or upset* (and the list goes on...) To be a spiritual seeker who also enjoys the pleasures of the world can be frowned upon leaving many of us 'in the closet' about living a modern day life whilst also following a spiritual path, and this guilt must stop.

I'd like to frankly address what a 'spiritual' person is upfront. From my experience, the stereotype is somebody you might find wearing crystals around their neck whilst chanting on a hilltop. After sitting at the dinner table at too many non-fat, non-meat, non-dairy dinner parties I had to wonder – *what is a spiritual person anyway?* Of course, I couldn't answer this question alone so I began to ask just about everybody what they believed made somebody spiritual and the answers I got were diverse and contained many of the buzzwords; *consciousness, connection, meditation, devotion* and *awareness.*

As much as I agree with all of that I can't help but believe that there is no template for a what a 'spiritual' person is, has or does. The Universe is not interested in that. Whatever you're showing as the most authentic is the highest spiritual expression of yourself possible. We do not have to choose between our human side and our spiritual side – we can have both. I don't believe that we should become consumed with trying to look like a "spiritual person" so much so that we abandon some of our most endearing and authentic traits. How many feel they have to trade in dairy for soy just to be spiritual? It may sound crazy but this actually happens. This doesn't serve anyone, especially when it's just for show.

If you feel overwhelmed by the so called list of things you need to do (or eat, or say, or wear just to fit in with the spiritual crowd), maybe these changes won't serve you.

I believe that when we begin to crave the fun and exciting things that we used to do, when those things fill our hearts with joy, the most spiritual thing we can do is lighten up and have some real fun that feeds our own soul. Maybe our favourite reality television show brings us joy, peace and relaxation.

Life is a spiritual practice. Avoiding life in pursuit of spirituality is impossible.

Perhaps watching football puts you in a euphoric trance where you lose track of time and place; who is to say that the joy you experience and the benefit of it is any different for your mental health than 15 minutes spent in meditation?

And I think sometimes one of the worst things about not being honest about your truth is the detriment caused when we might be encouraged not to show any sadness, anger, disappointment or hurt because that wouldn't be 'spiritual'. Why should we paint a huge fake smile on our faces just to ensure that nobody can see that we're not perfect, that we too can sometimes fall apart, make mistakes or feel hurt?

Showing up authentically is what makes us spiritual.

MAKING UP YOUR OWN MIND ABOUT YOUR UNIVERSE

The way you choose to relate to the higher power that you like and the way you see that connection is up to you. While I enjoy meditation centres and spiritual workshops, my favourite place to communicate with my higher power is at a coffee house. I'm not the only one on a Sunday morning gravitating in that direction to a good cup of coffee and who's to say that I'm not having a spiritual experience.

Years ago I heard an expression anywhere can *be your church*. Essentially, this means that you can find connection anywhere you go

When I was a teenager, I fell away from my religious faith and straight into the hands of spiritual practice. There seemed to be an ancient truth that dwelt within me, and it dwells within all of us, that is constantly calling us to live a life true to ourselves. I used to think that I was the only one who singled myself out to go in search of a higher meaning, but in my travels I've come to learn that it's not unusual to go on such a quest.

There doesn't appear to be a single culture alive on planet earth that hasn't searched for a higher meaning. In fact, we are all searching for meaning in our lives. It's the reason we do anything. Finding meaning in this world is the sole motivation behind any of our desires and aspirations. It's the reason we travel, the reason we love, and the reason we desperately seek approval and success.

We do all of this in an attempt to discover whose joke it was to place us on the planet in the first place and let us run free with very little idea of what we're actually doing. I figure that if you can't find meaning in the world then it becomes a scary place.

Maybe the reason why we can't find fulfilment around us is because we are already fulfilled in some way.

And once you find this truth and have faith that there is something bigger than you, the next question to answer is: *How do you communicate with it?*

The common answer is prayer. Not the kind of prayer that I was forced to say as a child in Ireland but a communication with the *something, somewhere, somehow.*

BECOMING A BETTER VERSION OF MYSELF

When I visited my meditation centre and asked Anika about prayer and how I should pray for the things I would like to have happen in my life she responded kindly; "Don't pray for a better life. Pray for a better *you.*"

A better me? What exactly did she mean? She could tell by my face I was a little puzzled by her statement so she explained herself in a way I could understand. "You don't need a better life, Seán," Anika said. "You need a better *mind.* Stop wanting all of the things you don't have and start wanting all of the things that you do have. A life that is only enjoyed in retrospect is an unfortunate one." She concluded and walked away.

I took a deep breath and wondered *had I never really been satisfied with my life?*

Almost immediately my inner guidance spoke up once again: "*Pray, meditate, become grateful, and enjoy your life a little bit more. Everything else will fall into place, my love.*"

With that knowledge I left the meditation centre I headed back to my apartment.

NOTES TO SELF:

1. Figure out your own views on God.

2. Visit a place of religious or spiritual devotion.

3. Decide on your own spiritual practice.

4. Learn to set clear intentions.

5. Don't pray for a better life. Pray for a better *self.*

Chapter 8

Embrace Your Inner Atheist

Call me crazy, but for my next stop towards spiritual enlightenment I have chosen to go in the complete opposite direction – Atheism.

Up to this point in my search for peace, happiness, and, dare I say it, divinity I had only been focussing on the devotees; the ones that really had faith and actively practiced connection to that something, somewhere, somehow.

But then I thought; what about the Atheists?

I wondered that there must be a way to exist in the world as a happy and peaceful individual even if you don't believe in that something, somewhere, somehow.

As much as it brought me immense comfort to sit in meditation and surrender myself to a happier feeling, I couldn't help but think that there was still a last bit of hesitation that existed within me. There was still a part of me that couldn't seem to fully believe how simplistic it all was and I wanted to explore the other side of the story. If I was going to take my spiritual practice seriously then I had to look at other paths.

When I thought about people who identified as Atheists, I questioned why some people devote their lives looking for a hidden meaning and others wouldn't accept it. I also wondered why some people go through difficult times only to feel closer to *God* and others go through equally hard times and conclude that *God* mustn't exist at all?"

I wanted to know more about this, even if it was just to satisfy my own personal curiosity.

What Exactly is an Atheist?

When I began to research it, it seems that an Atheist is usually defined as somebody who does not have belief in a God or gods, universal force, or anything anywhere that is bigger than us.

People maybe assume that an Atheist is somebody who has rejected all religion or spiritual doctrine and replaced it with negative and undesirable belief systems. But that's not true. Atheism can be the absence of belief and really doesn't have to do with the rejection of anything else. The word stems from the Greek word Atheos meaning 'without god(s)'.

Sometimes Atheists have a reputation of being *angry* people. But I don't think this is fair. It's very likely that in your life you will encounter some quite loving people who identify as Atheists and some very corrupt people who brand themselves as *extremely spiritual or religious.*

Alain de Botton, a respected British-based philosopher, has done a lot of work on the topic of atheism in his book *Religion For Athiests*. He reported that church attendance has been on a rapid decline and I too had noticed this when attending Sunday church services with my father.

As we sat quietly and the clock swiftly approached 9 a.m., my father turned around and noticed that the church was only marginally full compared to what it used to be like.

A CHURCH FOR NON-BELIEVERS

Through the wondrous powers of *meetup.com* I discovered a group in Hong Kong known as The Hong Kong Atheist Society. This seemed to be an active group of individuals who intended to push back against religious and spiritual influence. I got the impression that this group of Atheists didn't just passively allow the idea of religion to float by them, rather they felt compelled to fight back against people who do believe in God.

I reached for my computer and emailed its founding member: "Hello Peter: I'd love to talk to you about modern day spirituality and its influence. Thanks, Seán."

A few minutes later I received a reply: "Hello Seán, Give me a call any time about an interview on modern day spirituality. Peter."

That was a kind and welcome invitation and I didn't feel as if they were going to be hostile or aggressive toward me. Still I thought it best to keep my personal opinions of spirituality on the "down low" just for the moment.

Peter subsequently went on to invite me to join him at the weekly meeting of their group in Wan Chai district of Hong Kong. Wan Chai offered some of Hong Kong's most exciting nightlife and was also well known for its selection of strip clubs. Some may say it was a shady area, but it really was just a progressive strip of Hong Kong where expats would often gather in their thousands.

His email read: "Hello Seán, There are several groups here in Hong Kong based on the same idea - a lack of belief in the supernatural. A bunch of us are meeting this evening from 7:00 p.m. to at least 10:00 p.m. at a pub in Wan Chai. The only thing we all have in common is that we all speak English. The address is below. Come all the way to the back of the pub (as if you were going to the bathrooms) and look for me. I'm Caucasian and I have a shaved head. It's hard to miss me.

"It's quite loud there later in the evening but we can go to a local noodle shop for a more serious conversation afterwards. There will be many, many perspectives on spirituality at this event as there are members from all over the world and from all different religious backgrounds. Hope to see you there tonight. Peter."

LOSING MY RELIGION

I'd experienced warm nights in Hong Kong before, but the night I travelled across the city to meet the Atheists took things to a whole new level.

It was extremely humid.

I wandered up Lockhart Road that spans the entire length of Wan Chai from east to west and is over a mile long.

It seemed like a ten mile hike in that heat.

Finally arriving at the pub Peter had mentioned, I quickly ran inside to get a draft of air conditioning. As I began to dry off, a hand reached over and placed itself on my shoulder.

"Shaaaawwwwwn," a loud American voice greeted me.

"Yeah, you must be Peter," I said smiling.

"Let me get you a drink," he politely offered and then he headed to the bar returning to offer me a cold pint of Shandy, Peter jumped straight to the point.

"So it's awesome you want to talk about modern day spirituality," he said.

"Yeah, it's something I've been researching for a while now," I replied.

"And you feel like you've been lied to?" he asked.

Where did that come from? He was getting straight to the point.

"Erm ... erm ... no, I don't feel like I've been lied to," I replied.

Peter took a large gulp of his drink leaving me in suspense as to what he was going to say next. I feared he would bombard me with a practiced speech on anti-spiritual dogma or belittle my belief in something bigger than myself. But I was surprised and relieved by his response.

"That's cool man," he said. "You know, I don't believe in all of that stuff, manifestation and spirituality curing illness, but I've got huge respect for you if you do."

"Oh yeah?" I replied not unlike a little child.

Peter went on to explain. "You see, I used to be a cop and I always had one job to focus on and that was asking - *where's the evidence?*

"And you don't think you can find any evidence that backs up spiritual belief?", I queried.

"No. I don't think my mind is going to affect the external world and as far as I'm concerned, the sun revolves around the earth ... end of story."

I was a little blindsided and wasn't sure how to respond. Peter made it perfectly clear that we didn't share similar beliefs, but at least he was clear about it and non-judgemental of me.

I remember pausing for a brief second. I really admired his non-judgement. I have to admit that along my journey I have met spiritually superior people who would definitely judge Peter for his lack of belief, but contrary to this he just drank his beer and didn't concern himself too much with my beliefs.

"So would you say that even without belief you live a full life?" I asked with a bit of hesitation. "Of course I do.

I'm very happy and live a very full life. My life is my creed," he replied.

"And one final question," I posed. "What do you think happens when we die?"

Peter didn't have to think about his answer. "We blink out of existence," he replied with not the slightest hint of sadness, disappointment, or concern. I genuinely believed that he was a very happy person.

"Want another drink?" he asked me, as if I was just a regular friend in the crowded bar. *Which I guess I was.*

Downloading the Atheist Point of View

It turned out to be an enjoyable evening. I would never have expected to share an evening with an atheist in Hong Kong, but I rather enjoyed myself in spite of my initial fears of being judged.

It became clear to me that we are all looking for community and I'm actively interested in the ways in which people do this.

I doubted I would meet Peter again but I thanked him and moved toward the door back into the scorching heat.

As I approached a crossing I took a second to check in on my own beliefs. It was a good feeling not to have abandoned my spirituality but I did allow myself to question it and for me that was progress. I took the time to consider if I still believed everything I used to and I gave myself permission to let some older beliefs fall away.

I feel that through talking with him it actually helped me understand my beliefs more clearly. My faith was no longer blind and here's what I came to *know for sure:*

I happen to find peace and comfort in spirituality. I don't have to justify it, prove it to be true, or convince anyone else of it. This world is far too fragile for us not to seek comfort in something. When I meet someone who has found contentment of any kind, I'd be stupid to believe that I haven't got something to learn from them.

It's nobody else's job to believe what I believe – *it's my job* to believe what I believe. After all, I guess I'm not striving to be a more loving person to prove to some higher being that I can be. It's simpler than that. I'm striving to be more loving because it feels good when I do. That's that. *I think.*

HOLDING MY BELIEFS UNDER THE MICROSCOPE

So my conclusion from that meeting in Wan Chi?

It was that any belief is fine with me. If you want to experience peace on your own terms, choose something you can believe in and go for it.

Ask yourself this: *What I am thinking and believing that is bringing unease into my life?* Could it be that we might be stuck with old thoughts and limiting beliefs and it is time to move on from those? It could be a big relief.

It can be hard to let go of old beliefs though. As humans we have a tendency to believe anything we think, especially if we find ourselves thinking it often enough. Ideas and beliefs become embedded in our psyche over time. But it's actually a kind of arrogance of the ego that makes this happen. It's easier just to accept what you have always accepted, rather than stopping to actually question if what you believe is really true.

I was fascinated to read that researchers have discovered that humans have about 70,000 thoughts per day. Can you seriously tell me that every one of us has a 100% accuracy rate with our thoughts?

That's almost a thought every second so somewhere your brain has to mess up with an untruth every now and then. But here's what I figured out. You can decide to question your beliefs, even if they are deeply engrained. We are all scientists by nature; within our lives and experiences. We can question and change anything we want to.

We live much of our lives by trial, error and probability. We have collected a lot of data in our heads. In fact, you've been collecting data since the day we were born. *If I cry, they will come and help me. I shouldn't touch fire because it's hot. Last time I spoke in public, I felt uncomfortable so let's not do that again.*

All that does make sense but with our emotional life and experiences the data and the recordings are not always that clear or correct. We can be missing data and therefore find it hard to form conclusions in our daily lives and so we sometimes make up stories just because we can't abide by the idea of missing pieces to a puzzle.

This draws me to the question: *What stories am I making up about my life that make me unhappy?*

This was particularly relevant to me considering how miserable I once felt. I could see that it mainly came down to my being convinced that the path I was on would never change.

Now ask yourself this last question: *Without what I'm thinking and believing, am I okay?*

Damn, if only I had this process of inquiry* when I was hiding under my bed covers.

All of a sudden you realise that you might not need all those old beliefs and you really can question them. Maybe questioning your beliefs or letting some go entirely is the true path to enlightenment.

*For more work in the field of thoughts and inquiry I highly recommend exploring the work of Byron Katie by visiting www.TheWork.com

ANYONE CAN CHANGE THE WORLD (SO SIT YOUR SPIRITUAL ASS DOWN)

I want to share a story with you about the night my friend Lan Hei, who was a reporter for cable TV, celebrated her 26th birthday. She had chosen to gather the entire TV network in a backroom of a thirtieth floor nightclub for karaoke. I was lucky to be one of those people and I happily sipped on the free bubble gum cocktails and sang along to some classics.

Just a few hours afterwards (devoid of sleep) I met my friend Sophia to explore the Ladies Street Market in Mong

Kok. Mong Kok is not a place you visit casually as it requires a relentless determination just to make it through the crowds. There were more than a hundred stalls selling bargain clothing, cosmetics, jewellery, and souvenirs but we somehow survived the stampede of shoppers and made it to the safe haven of a coffee house.

I was exhausted and Sophia also looked pretty damn shitty. She weakly lifted her hands to her mouth to quench her need for caffeine, sipping from her small cup of coffee. "What's up with you?" I asked and her face showed three confusing and contradictory messages: something was definitely wrong, she didn't want to get into it and she was going to tell me anyway.

Turns out, Sophia was on the phone the previous night to her friend Rowena in the Philippines. Rowena was a mother of two whom Sophia had met while volunteering at an orphanage. Rowena had fallen on hard times. She had no money and couldn't afford to feed her children. Thus Sophia was troubled. In fact, she was pissed off.

At what? The injustice, corruption and discrimination that caused the issue. Though this topic of conversation seemed a little heavy for afternoon coffee, we were already jumping in and putting the world to rights. Sophia studied politics at university and I have a lot to learn from her. She knew far more than I did about foreign aid, international relations and overseas affairs. In fact she was a fountain of knowledge and passion.

The conversation of spirituality and politics is a vast one. It's probably a whole other book, so I won't dive into that. I will say this. It surprises me that so many people who practice spirituality steer clear of politics and world news. They may be in pursuit of healing themselves, but not the world. I personally believe that it's a disservice to the name of spirituality to only use its universal forces for personal gain.

But here was Sophia. She would not call herself a spiritual person. I don't think she has ever meditated in her life, and I doubted the she even believed in a higher power. But it didn't matter. On that day, Sophia had decided to transfer some of her own money to Rowena so she could buy food for her children for the next few weeks while seeking out aid from her government in the Philippines.

I was very much in awe of Sophia. Her commitment to acts of kindness in the world outweighs whatever she might profess to believe or not believe. She taught me that spirituality is not just something *you are* it's something *you do*. If you ask me, forget about her being spiritual; she's a saint.

FINDING MY OWN CHURCH IN A STARBUCKS

You know why I believe in God? *Green tea iced latte.*

One day whilst I was in my spiritual home of Starbucks I felt that I was beginning to feel spiritual burnout; I had been up all weekend taking extra meditation time at the Raja Yoga Centre due to a visit guru from India – her meditations started at 5am. I had been reading nothing but spiritual texts and taking any belief that came my way as gospel – even if only for a short time. I had decided that I had to get up from my meditation pillow and not ignore the fun and mystery this city had to offer. I remember feeling at the time that I was 'taking a break from God' by sampling amazing food, partying on the beach, and watching light shows on the rooftops? Turns out I was wrong.

Seems like I was actually getting closer to God.

NOTES TO SELF:

1. Have a conversation with an Atheist.

2. Abstain from all spiritual practice for one week and see which ones you miss and only keep doing those.

3. Write a list of something causing you stress and explore it

4. Meet up with a local community group (I recommend meetup.com)

5. Do for others, as you would like them to do for you.

Chapter 9

Go ahead; forgive it all and let it go.

There is something beautiful about endings. It's a time where you allow yourself to stop and take stock of the lessons, the moments, and the beautiful incidences gone by.

From the time I first landed in Hong Kong to the end of my visit there, I experienced a vast number of life-changing events. I'd been for coffee on my own, posed as an athiest, meditated about five hundred times, stood at the feet of a 100-foot Buddha, and learned the Islamic prayer routine. It's safe to say that even if that was the full extent of my experiences I would have been forever changed.

However, I knew there was one last thing I had to do before I returned home.

Forgive.

Damn it.

I knew I had to make peace with my past otherwise I would only go on to live the same life back in Liverpool as I had before my Southeast Asian journey. I wasn't entirely sure how I was going to do this but I knew it had to be done.

Even with what I know now, forgiveness is a peculiar concept. You may need to forgive a person, a situation, a group of people, a past experience, a past event, or like me, maybe you also might need to forgive yourself. To put it simply, forgiveness is necessary for anything you think back on and causes you to get knots in your stomach.

Sure, in Hong Kong I had felt totally at peace as I sat in my meditation class and even when I was sipping those heavenly green tea lattes at Starbucks with a friend. However it was in those moments when I was walking home alone that I remembered the person who hurt me, the person who didn't value me, the person who had embarrassed me, and the life situation that didn't go the way I wanted, so much so that I would almost keel over with stomach pain.

I could vividly remember the times I didn't stand up for myself and the times I was a doormat. If you scratched away at my spiritual surface, standing there thinking about my life, you would have found my shame that I had tried so hard to keep so well hidden.

I hated the fact that it was still there. It felt like it was lurking. Waiting. Ready to sabotage me all over again.

THE PROCESS OF REAL FORGIVENESS

People tend to think of forgiveness as a verb, something else we have to *do*.

However, I think that forgiveness is a little beyond action; it's either something you feel or you don't. You can't trick yourself into pretending that you've forgiven someone.

Still I believe that we all truly want to forgive and there are things we can do to get closer to the feeling of forgiveness.

Even if we don't want to forgive at first after we have spent days, weeks and years on end being filled with anger and resentment, in our hearts we truly want to forgive because we don't have to feel the pain anymore. We often come to the point of forgiveness when we drop any plans for revenge and when we want to stop brooding over past hurts that just don't make sense to keep around anymore.

There are times in my life when I have told myself that I had forgiven somebody but the very thought of them still made me sick. That was not forgiveness. That was denial and it's an on-going lesson. People seem to pop up left, right and centre with the sole intention just to piss us off – this is never going to be easy.

Learning to forgive will make you a much more resilient person.

There were even times when I boasted about my forgiveness of somebody because it made me feel *spiritually superior* to be so able to forgive but I wasn't kidding anybody but myself. I knew these points of forgiveness weren't real because when you truly forgive, you can think back to that situation or person with it having little effect on you.

I believe that true forgiveness is the key element that ties all spiritual practice together thus that is why I have made it this last chapter and likely why The Universe made it one of my last internal adventures on this trip. It's impossible to strive for a happier life without letting go of a hell of a lot from your past. You may try to avoid forgiveness by taking on an extra yoga class, getting another Reiki healing, or going gluten-free – but after the class, the treatment or the meal you'll still be faced with your same old thoughts.

Making Sense of the Future by Looking Backwards

When I look back on my own life, there seemed to be a pattern I would follow in my life: I was drawn to people who didn't value me. Don't get me wrong, I had good friends but many of the people I tended to hang out with tied me to my past, and held me back when I tried to explore new things.

Despite the fact I was smart enough to realise this was going on, I still went to the ends of the earth to gain the approval of these people. I would host group dinners only to find myself the only one not involved in the conversation and paying for bottles of wine that I didn't drink. At times it even felt like I was the most unwelcome person in my own home.

It didn't feel like that I had that many friends despite being constantly surrounded by people. It was grounds for much confusion. I rarely had a day where I came home from work and spent time alone or engaged in hobbies and activities that I actually enjoyed. Before these low points, I used to enjoy taking classes and I had even won few stand-up comedy competitions. Inevitably my self-confidence had taken a dive I didn't have the energy or enthusiasm for anything but the bare minimum when it came to my own self.

In retrospect, I can see that was the classic example of a doormat. Despite my previous efforts to change, it was clear that I was somewhat held hostage by that particular circle of acquaintances, the ones who constantly echoed my own thoughts: "This is your life, get used to it. You're not getting out of here. This is how it will always be. You'll never be invited to the fun and joy that everybody else seems to be having."

ALLOW YOURSELF TO FEEL HOW YOU FEEL

I wasn't entirely in tune with my inner world and guidance at this point in my life so I couldn't intellectually fathom why I was growing sadder and sadder by the day. After about six months of bad company, countless dismally unpleasant dinner parties, and catastrophic attempts at having a fun night out, I was not only feeling depressed but also I was mad as hell.

It turns out that anger is a key emotion in the forgiveness equation. It tends to come after we feel desperately sorry for ourselves. If we fail to express that anger, get it out in some healthy way, then we stay stuck within an ongoing cycle of mad-as-hell.

I was very much like all the other people pleasers out there. There just wasn't' any way to express my anger and I found myself stuck between sad and angry with no way out: I would go from sad to angry, back to sad and then back to angry. It didn't feel like it was my fault but there I was. To be honest, I was in complete denial about how angry and disappointed I actually was and the resentment kept growing daily.

When the chance to travel to Hong Kong came up it lifted me out of the anger and resentment but it didn't remove the anger and resentment from my system. Each day I spent in Hong Kong, I felt better as I learned so many ways to live a happier and healthier life. I was turning into a new person, an improved version of myself, but I still needed to be more secure before heading back to my previous life or I knew I would fall apart again under the pressure of merely living in the modern world.

I had to learn to forgive, otherwise I dreaded that my entire journey would have been just for fun and distraction and would be void of any true transformation.

TIME TO TAKE A DEEP BREATH; IT'S TIME TO FORGIVE

The time had come for me to partake in a ritual that expats in Hong Kong appear to call a *phenomenon*. I was going to hike to Ham Tim Wan Beach and spend the night on its glorious sand.

This expedition is almost like a rite of passage for first-time visitors to Hong Kong, but it's not something listed in the tourist brochures. It's a little like a club. You need to know somebody who has already done it who will invite you along and luckily my friend Moose invited me along for a weekend in the sand. Of course I was a little apprehensive about spending the night camping on the beach, until I thought about the thousands who did it before me, and they seemed to think that it was a marvellous idea so I was willing to go along.

I packed my blanket, a change of clothes, water and my iPod. I honestly didn't know what was appropriate to pack. It was exciting to me that I was going to experience an amazingly different side of the city of Hong Kong. It wasn't just a concrete jungle and business town. In fact, there are corners of Hong Kong where you could hide out and *never* be found. This was actually comforting.

During the five-mile journey to the beach, we trekked over sandy paths, green mountains, under bridges, past deserted restaurants, and through tight passages. Eventually we were forced to use our final smidge of exertion up a steep set of one thousands steps finally leading us to our utopia.

I know that I'm a writer and somehow should be able to paint a vivid picture of this beach through analogies, adjectives and explanations. However I worry that anything I say would only be an injustice to the *fantasy* that was before me, so instead I will allow you to picture for yourself the most perfect beach surrounded by cliffs and ask you to keep that image in mind.

As for us, we just took a deep gasp and began to run toward our paradise. We descended onto this golden glory like an army, each of us wearing a pair of aviator sunglasses and carrying an overnight bag on our back. We swiftly marked our territory in a small section of this sanctuary and begin to set up home for the night. There were only about three friendship groups camping out here on this occasion so we each inhabited what seemed like our own personal section of the beach.

As I attempted to erect a fragile tent, clearly highlighting to all of my peers that I had never done such a thing before, I came to consider that I was infinitely lucky. Less than one year before this, I had to wrestle with all of my strength just to get out of bed and here I was with plans to stay up all night and swim in the ocean at sunrise.

We lit a campfire. We sang acoustic versions of pop songs. We drank. We ate. We got warm.

The sun was setting and I found myself gravitating towards the ocean. I stayed about twelve feet away from the tide and dug my feet in the sand and sat down wrapping my arms around my knees. Everything felt so *right*. It was not necessarily the happiest I've ever felt or the most enlightened, but something in the air told me that everything *was* okay and it *had always been* okay. That even in my times of sadness, anxiety and fear The Universe has pre-mapped out little rejuvenation spots for me where I could recharge and heal. I took a deep breath and allowed the ocean breeze to seep into my lungs and then it occurred to me:

This was my big moment.

It was time that I let all of my shit from the past go.

The soft subtle voice of inner guidance instructed me: "Go ahead, forgive it all. Let it go. It's time."

I didn't shy away from uncomfortable urges in my body. I recalled the pain and felt it. I allowed my memories to mirror the action of the ocean ahead of me. *Ebb and flow. Come and go. Happy and sad.* It's all good.

I made a mental note to myself at this point that I still think about when I need to keep perspective and keep on forgiving: "You did the best you could. They did the best they could. It wasn't perfect but it was good enough to bring you here. You'll never fully understand your own strength but you'll always be strong enough. You don't know why it happened but it happened, so call it a fond memory or an uncomfortable remembrance and let it go. It's over now. The past is over, the sun has set and a new day has come. You are starting over today equipped with all you'll ever need."

Before I got back up from my crouch-like position, a thought from The Universe entered my mind: *Take a deep breath. It's all behind you now.*

There is no doubt that I started to feel lighter. Not in a physical way but I moved around my daily chores with greater ease. I was happy to be me and be in my own skin.

Maybe this isn't how I felt every second of every day, but whenever I would summon or feel even the slightest glimpse into that beautiful peaceful feeling it was enough to fuel me for days on end.

My final days in Hong Kong were spent with an overwhelming sense of inner joy, the kind a child feels most days where nothing spectacular has to happen but with a sense of everything that's happening is*spectacular* in its own way.

A LESSON IN JUST *Being*

I was blessed and saddened to take in one final meditation at the Raja Yoga Centre in Tin Hau and one concluding cup of green tea with my teacher before I boarded my plane. We sat at the reception desk at the front of the building next to its gigantic glass front. The orange walls of this building seemed more vibrant to me in that moment and the dim lighting felt warmer to me than it ever had before.

As far as I was aware, this quite likely would be my last time seeing my teacher so I was ensuring that I took in every little last detail.

"Are you excited to return home?" Devi asked me.

"I am," I replied.

"You will always take the lessons of Raja Yoga with you?" she sternly asked, like a teacher ensuring that I would do my homework.

"Of course I will," I laughed.

"You are love, you are joy, you are peace, you are knowledge, you are mercy, you are bliss. Don't forget that."

"I won't."

"We will meet again," she said.

"I really hope so," I answered.

"One final lesson for this trip," she told me and I became very intrigued. "See the drama in your life as mere entertainment."

"So you know I'm somebody who flourishes in drama?" I ask.

"I know you're somebody who used to be that way," she answered. I smiled.

"You're going to be just fine," she said as she placed her hand over mine. There was no need for any words or gestures. There was just being.

"See you again," Devi said again with certainty.

I hope so, I whispered to myself.

ONE FINAL ROOFTOP

On the last day with my friends and my newly found family, I heard a small echoing in the background, and then realised it was a friend. "Seán, can you come with me for a second?" It was one of my friends Jane calling me to follow her.

Without being able to question this instruction or ask what was up, I began to chase after her. She was moving so fast that she became a blur in the distance. I continued to trail behind her and began to climb the outdoor concrete stairs of this old and beautiful Hong Kong building we were in.

Now, I had walked up this stairway a few hundred times before, however today the steps seemed to be endless as if all I would find at the end of one flight of steps was another and another. I wondered if I had fallen into some kind of quantum physics *Wonderland* where all previous understanding of my surroundings had been suspended. This felt very strange to me and in this moment, everything became hazy. As I continue to climb higher and higher, Jane seemed to be moving more and more quickly and this caused my confused emotions to intensify.

Finally we reached the top of the building and I struggled to catch my breath. Moose fiercely and unapologetically trespassed onto the property next door by breaking through a fire-exit door and leading us into a bright yellow light and onto an extravagant Hong Kong rooftop.

Even on this late December day the sun was blinding. Every step I took I felt like a touch of grace. I could not mistake the soft breeze for anything less than a personal handshake from The Universe. With every sacred second, I enjoyed the astonishing, yet subtle sensations of insecurity, resentment and hurt dissolve into the sunlight.

I felt as if I had acquired the superpower of 360 degree vision as I looked out for miles on the city that had rescued me from my self-loathing and firmly carried me into a place of more self-love then I had ever known before. In that moment I knew that The Universe had saved me; it seems like it paused the entire world just to ensure I could feel this sensation of grace. Surprisingly, in the midst of all of this beauty, the predominate feeling that arose within me was not that of overwhelming gratitude but something more subtle. It was as if The Universe was the one feeling grateful, as if all The Universe has ever wanted for me was this feeling of bliss. I could hear The Universe breathing a sigh of relief that I was finally embracing all of who I was, certainly more than I ever had done before.

I realised that on that rooftop there was little, if anything, between me and The Universe. In fact, there's always little, if anything, between me and The Universe. In that moment, I realised that it didn't matter if I believed in miracles or not. No matter what I do, *miracles believe in me.*

I took a seat next to Moose on a wooden bench frighteningly close to the edge of the rooftop. There was silence, not something I found much of while living in this pulsating city.

I continued to find it hard to catch my breath as I allowed this feeling of pure grace inhabit my entire body. An almost haunting realisation overcame me as I began to recognize that this same feeling of heavenly comfort had visited me before.

That day in Liverpool as I crossed the street. And then the message came again. Maybe a message from The Universe, maybe from some inner guidance, or maybe just a thought of my own.

Whatever the source, I heard quite clearly: *"You see, I told you to stick around long enough for something good to happen"*

True Story.

Final Note to Self: I am Enough

As I look behind me to that journey I took when I was twenty two years old, I feel an overwhelming desire to travel back in time and console my younger, messed-up, anxious self. I wish I could let him know that somewhere along this crazy road of life and trying to survive in twenty-first-century living he will find peace. I know now that he'll find not only peace but a creative and fulfilling vocation, he'll continue to travel, and he'll enjoy a lifetime of continuing to meet incredibly awesome and inspiring people along the way.

My lessons and journeys (and of course setbacks) didn't stop the day I landed back on British soil. In fact, when I look back now, I accept that my time in Hong Kong merely scratched the surface of what would become a life-long journey where I would truly learn to understand how spirit works, how life unfolds, and of course, I continue every day to learn about *myself.*

When I returned home, I founded my company *That Guy Who Loves The Universe.* It started out as a Facebook fan page where I have the pleasure of sharing my daily musings on life, spirit and wellness. The audience for my work has since grown to more than 20,000 people and it has allowed me to travel to many more places in the world that I have come to love dearly, and each of those places also had something to teach me about myself.

Specifically I have loved my further adventures in Los Angeles where I have continued to live out my dreams of driving down the 101 in a convertible and adopt the chilled out lifestyle that California has to offer. No longer do I feel like the lost waif who was stranded at a chaotic and soul-deadening pool party. Now I get to enjoy my trips with a full heart and in good company. I even got to write this, my first book, which has been an incredible adventure in and of itself.

All of this being said, as wonderful as it is, I've continued to stay well acquainted with *setbacks* but now I have learned to accept them as inevitable roadblocks that are just a sign of the fact I am moving forward in my life. Have I *only* met people who have wished me well? *Of course not.* There are still some difficult people out there of course who are angry and jealous perhaps, but every day I'm learning to focus more and more on the people who are seeking their best.

As I continue to travel along this path, I hope that I can be an example for somebody else to raise them up so they can believe that they too are capable and deserving of better things. We all are.

Since my Southeast Asian excursion, I have earned my Master's degree in Psychology and I'm continuing to explore the field of study concerned with Positive Psychology, Flourishing and Spiritual Intelligence. I've also come to learn a lot about mental health, especially my own. I know that no matter how much of a spiritual life I continue to live, I fully anticipate that there will be times my heart will break and I'll grieve for peace and joy. The difference moving forward is that I've learned not to take this all so seriously and I try not to let my brain get sick the same way my body sometimes does. Yes, sometimes I still catch a cold and some winters, I feel down. This is all part of my spiritual journey.

Another reason I feel more positive in general is because I've come to learn that a meaningful life is not a popularity contest. Although I enjoy Facebook 'likes' and Instagram followers, I've learned not to allow my career to have more attention or to be more exciting than my life itself.

Because I don't want to miss out on even the small things. *Ever.*

That's why I expect the next phase of my life will be my second chance to really take a moment and drink it all in. I'll never forget the immense joy that I once felt by drinking beer on a Hong Kong rooftop and detecting, even ever so slightly, that the entire Universe had been given just to me, so I could somehow find a little more peace.

What do I see for myself in the future? Honestly with every day that dawns, I feel more and more taken hostage by *Love*. Not in a gooey or fluffy way, but every day my heart opens up a little bit more to the complexity and beauty of the human experience. I am continuously filled with compassion that we are all just doing our best to navigate our way through this crazy world. I'll enjoy continuing to contribute to the spiritual movement that is happening all over the world by writing books, teaching classes, meditating daily, and meeting-up with some wonderful people for coffee.

My advice to you, wonderful one, is to take your dreams and run with them. They may not even make sense to you at the time, but the clearer you get, the more you'll be able to follow your bliss with conviction. I strongly encourage you to find a connection with that *something, somewhere, somehow* which can comfort you through life's up and downs. Please find a way to accept that there is a cosmic force at play that loves you more than you could possibly know.

Finally, I'd say that when you've done all that you can do, when you've tried to control all that you can control, when you've just about hurt all that you can hurt, when you've given everything you've got and when you're tired of situation after situation, let go and turn ward, *turn inward.*

Your peace was there all along.

All my love to you,

From Seán and from The Universe!

Acknowledgments

This book would not have been possible without a few people who I would like to thank;

Mum, *firstly* thank you for being neither poor nor unfortunate but most of all thank you for always allowing me to explore where I fitted into the world. We can both agree it's not been easy but it's definitely been worth it.

To the rest of my close family: Dad, Emma, Melissa & Anita, Sarah, Steve, Ben & Sam. I'm so grateful to be part of such an open and loving family. The older we all get the more we become a close knit group of friends and that means the world to me.

To the *Craven Crew at No. 1*; thank you for letting me live with you for almost three years whilst I focused on this book in the background. Without you guys there may not be a book.

To Pete. You have been such a support for this entire project and held my hand through the final stages. I am so grateful. You have given your time and energy to make this book the best it can be and I am so grateful.

To my wonderful editors and friends; the powerhouse that is Jo Fisher & Kirsty Rothwell. Thank you for the long days of hard work you put into this book. I'm excited for our future adventures together.

For Maisie, you have been there for the past two years of this books creation and encouraged me creatively more than you could possibly know. May we always continue to humour in our creativity inklings and be brave enough to see where they lead.

Kate, thank for not only being *a friend of the year* but a friend of a lifetime. I have no doubt that between us we can keep each other entertained with stories of life's funny twists and turns for all of eternity. I hope that neither of us ever fully *get it together* – where would the good stories come from?

Lucy, you have not only been my friend but my pro bono therapist for the past five years. It's the most reassuring thing in the world to me that there is somebody I can always turn to where I don't need to censor my thoughts or words. May we never have any private thoughts when we are with each other.

Sara, you have been my #1 cheerleader from day one. Thank you for speaking up about my accomplishments when I am too shy to do so and always reassuring me that *it's worth it* even when I want to give up.

For my mentors: Robert Holden & Gabby Bernstein. Thank you for seeing something in me that I couldn't always see in myself. You have helped me more than you could know.

For Leigh Daniel, founder of Project Positive Change. Thank you for seeing something in me and inviting me to come and work with you. I have immensely enjoyed our road trips around the US and envision many more in our future.

Throughout the writing of this book I have worked in some wonderful organisations; I would like to thank all of those who I have ate lunch with, danced with, drank with put the world to rights with from National Museums

Liverpool, St. Chads High School and the University of Liverpool.

Last but by no means least; I would like to extend the most sincere and heartfelt thank you to all of the Universe Lovers from my facebook page That Guy Who Loves The Universe. I know you come from far and wide; India, Africa, Malaysia Mexico, UK, US, UAE, Romania, Indonesia, France, Italy, Norway (and the list goes on). Over the past five years I have shared some of my most private and intimate thoughts and experiences with you always to be met with comfort and open arms. It is my pleasure to be invited into your lives to spread a little joy. For all of those who have commented and messaged me saying that I have 'changed your life' – I have to be completely upfront and say that it is *in fact* you who has changed my life. Having an audience to share my work with is the greatest gift I could have ever asked for and you are the sole reason why there is any of this. Thank You

Join the Community

To join the community please visit
facebook.com/ThatGuyWhoLovesTheUniverse

Printed in Great Britain
by Amazon